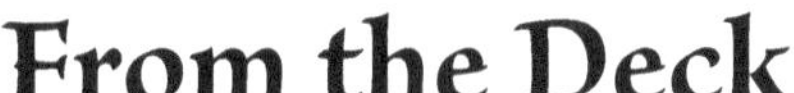

From the Deck

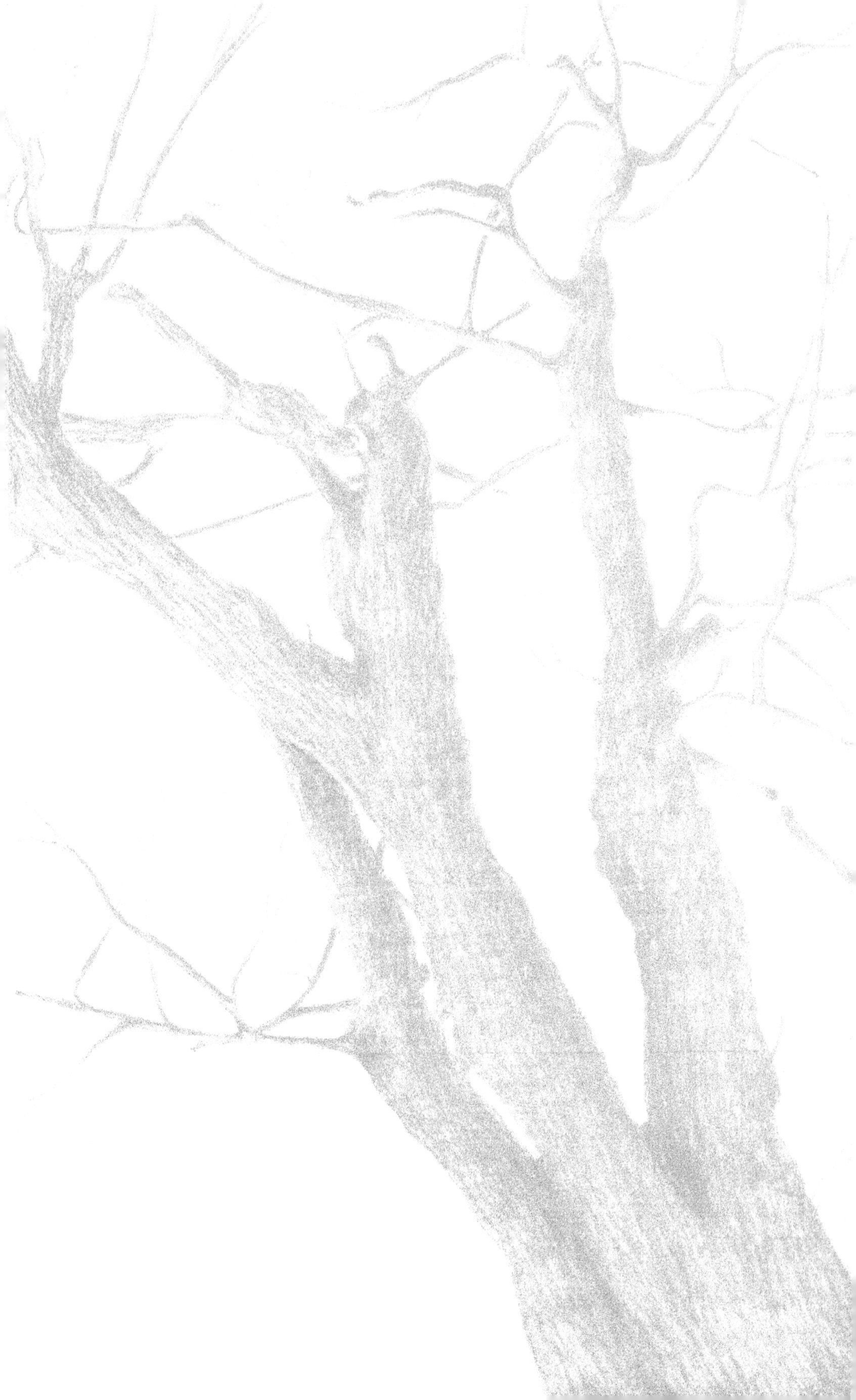

From the Deck

POETRY BY

Robert Brennan

EASTON, CONNECTICUT

This volume is published by OctoberWorks, 2024

Designed and set in Brioso Pro
by Jeanne Criscola | Criscola Design, North Haven, Connecticut.
Printed in the United States of America by IngramSpark.

Library of Congress Control Number: 2024914975
ISBN: 978-1-959262-08-4

———

CHARCOAL DRAWINGS BY ROBERT BRENNAN

COVER *From the Deck*
PAGE 14 *The Witness*
PAGE 18 *Solitary Maple*
PAGE 208 *Winter Light*

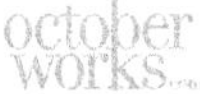

Dedication

This book is dedicated to the memory of my beloved daughter Robin, who shared with each of us the joys, sadness, and challenges of being human. With great generosity, she was the first to give me my first journals and, more importantly, an encouragement to write.

Robin, no words can capture my sadness in your leaving us too soon.

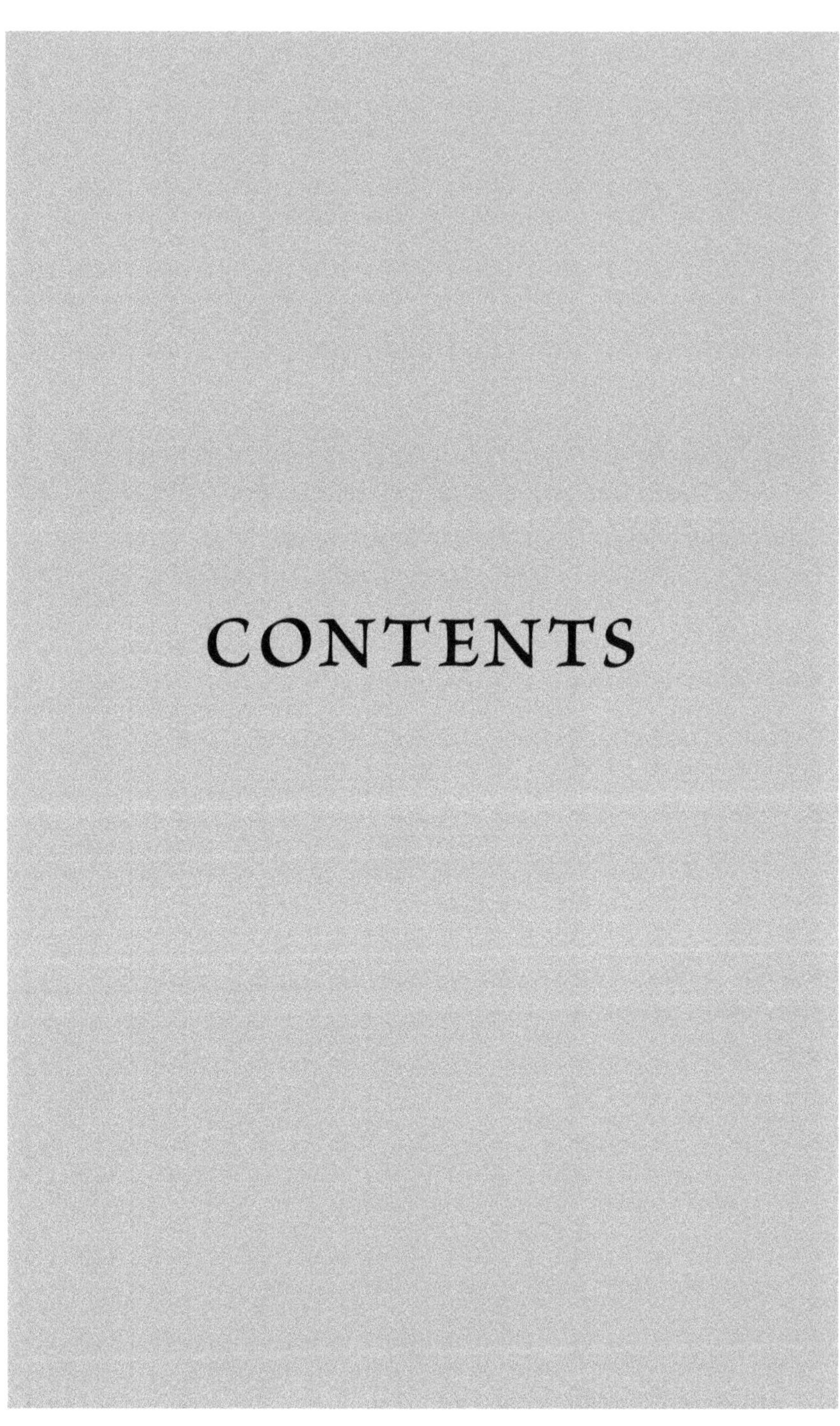

CONTENTS

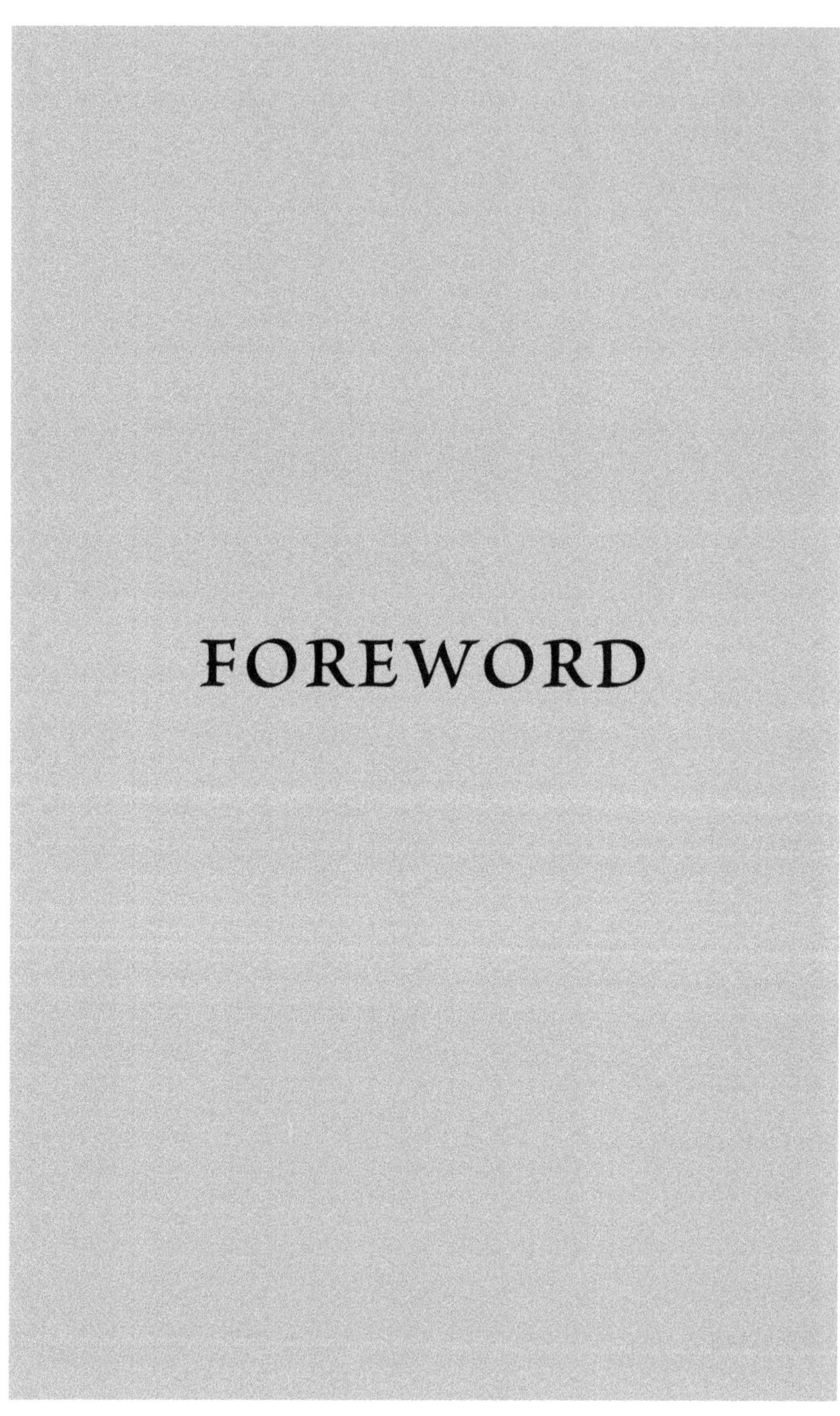

FOREWORD

Robert Brennan examines our world with a restless eye. He takes in a fractal view, filled with the minutia of elements. Sights and sounds and abstract concepts have all been explored throughout a long and distinguished career in his manifold styling of art. Whether looking from the deck (at the helm) of his sailing boat, from the deck of his studio overlooking the New England landscape, or in a state of quiet solitude, his restless eye misses nothing. As it is with his art, so it is with his poetry. Robert writes with the spare and elegant profundity of an antique soul, his finger placed squarely on our corporeal and spiritual existential pulse.

From The Deck is not merely a collection of poems. It is an invitation to witness a dance of words and images, orchestrated by a masterful visual artist. In the quiet spaces between brush-stroked words and inked lines, there lies a subtext where color and language converge, revealing a realm of boundless expression, a conduit to the universe seeking the obvious that so often remains unnoticed.

To say that the poems contained in this volume are eclectic is a vast understatement. It is a variegated tumble of emotions and ideas that flow like a musical improvisation. Like Robert's visual art, this poetry defies categorization. One moment, you'll find yourself lost in the swirling eddies of irony; the next, you'll be hurtling through the jagged, fractured landscape of a modernist experiment. It is a reflection of Robert's restless eye, always

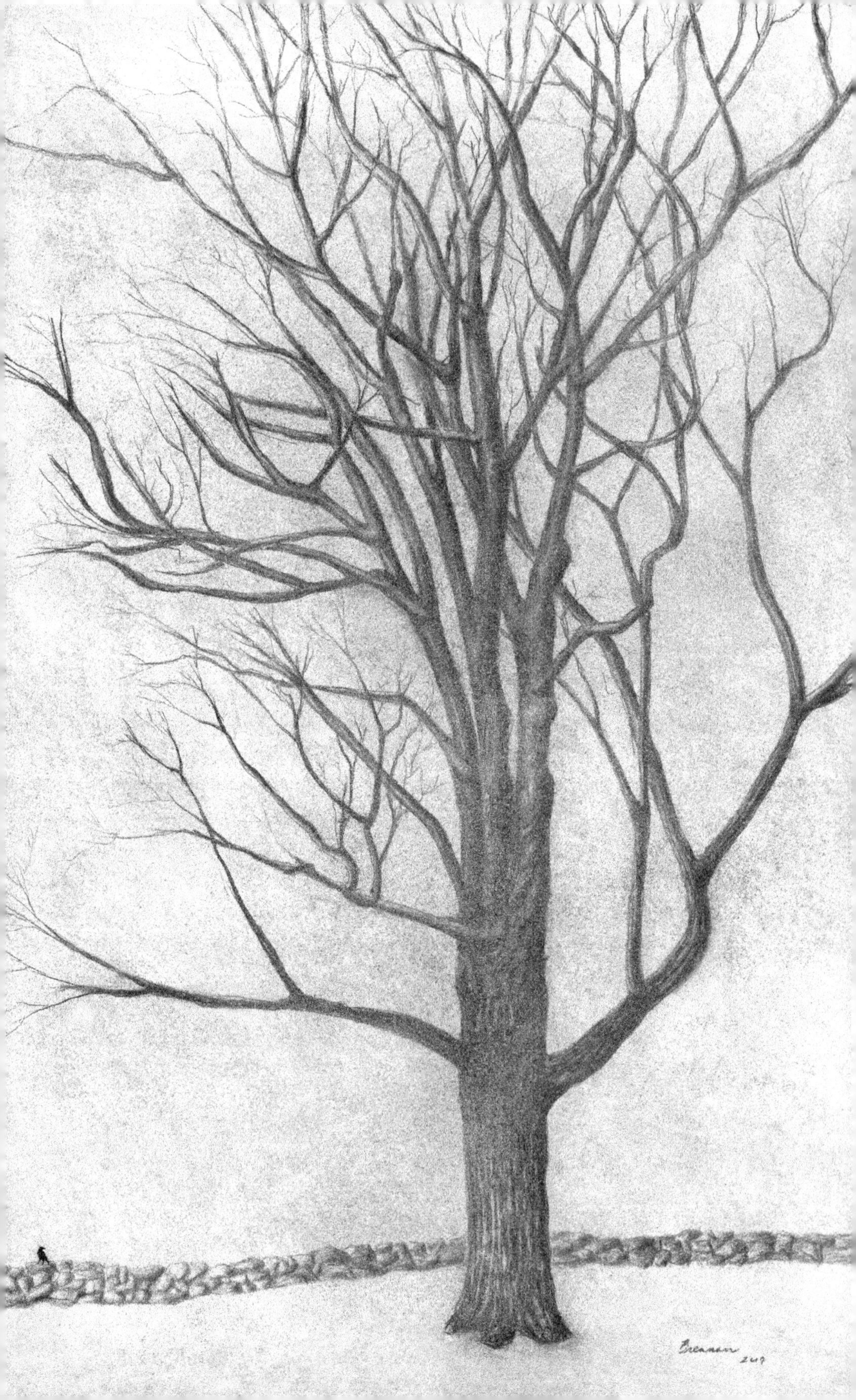

seeking out the unexpected, the sublime in the mundane, wise and witty and profoundly moving.

Gentle Reader, may you discover your own canvas within these lines, waiting for your colors, your stories, your art. This is a collection you will be returning to time and time again.

KIT BRINER

Dramaturge
Easton Arts Council Actor/Director
Playwright

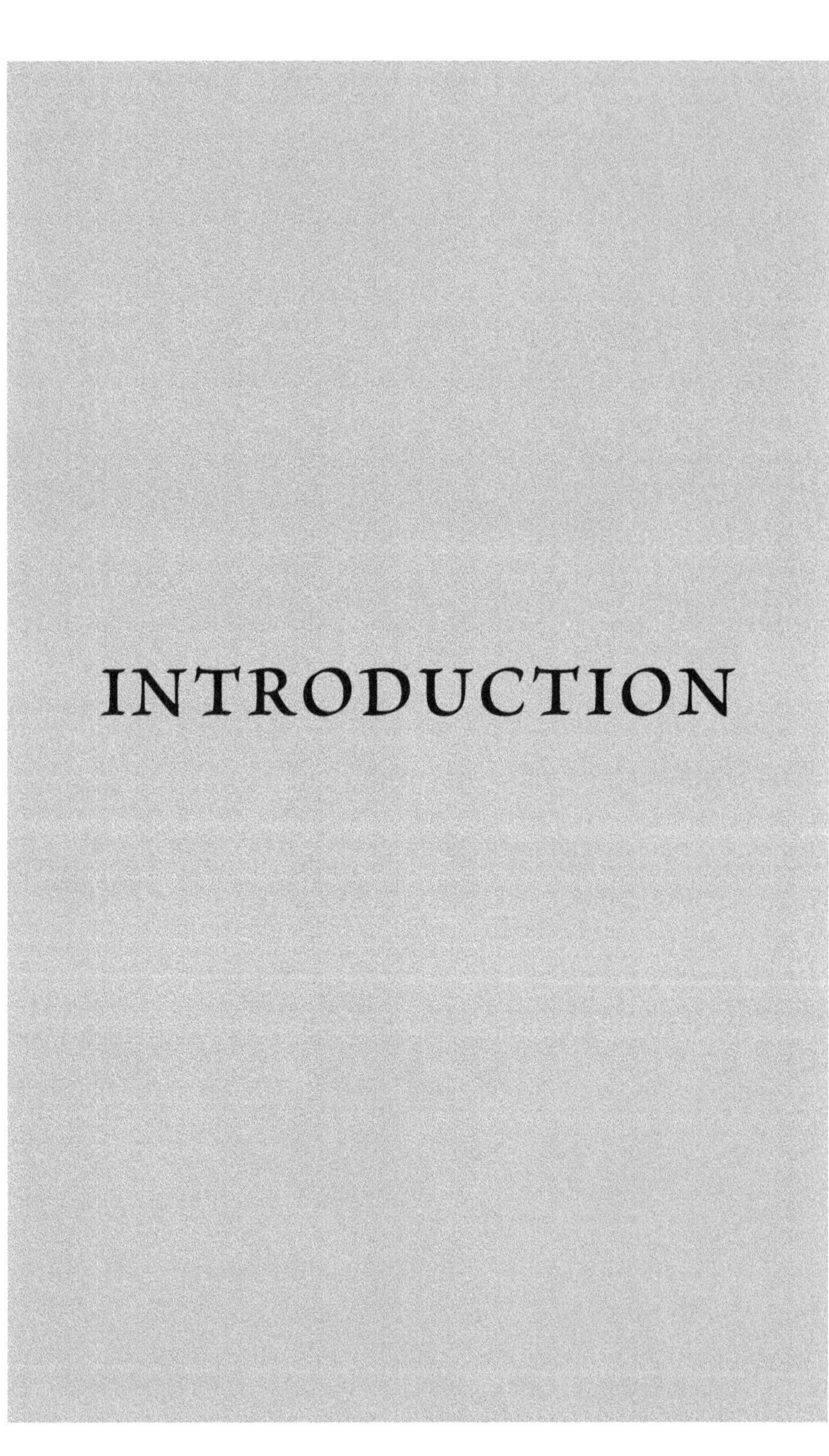

INTRODUCTION

COUNTLESS SCHEMES for organizing this book have come and gone: themes, perhaps, those about nature, followed by comments on the plights of mankind, love, sadness, humor, politics, and others.

Upon reflection, I realized that such an order did not reflect the characteristics of how I write or how I think or, in fact, how the world unfolds before my eyes. In truth, my afternoon walk along the road that has inspired words about aging against a sunset differ from those inspired by the moving in and out of sadness in the evening news.

As in everyman's mind, the flow is steady and varied and punctuated by moments of lucidity and wonder, by moments of fear and anguish and peacefulness and great sorrow and all elements of human thinking and feeling.

Still, while each of us experiences periods in our lives of prolonged states of mind and heart, as when we are heartbroken over the loss of a loved one, life in its totality is — for good or for bad — a moving screen.

This book is not arranged in categories. There might be pages near each other that are similar in content and tone. In other cases, the subject from one page to the next might be radically different. It is intended that each page stands on its own, which again, for good or bad, more faithfully reflects how my poems arise.

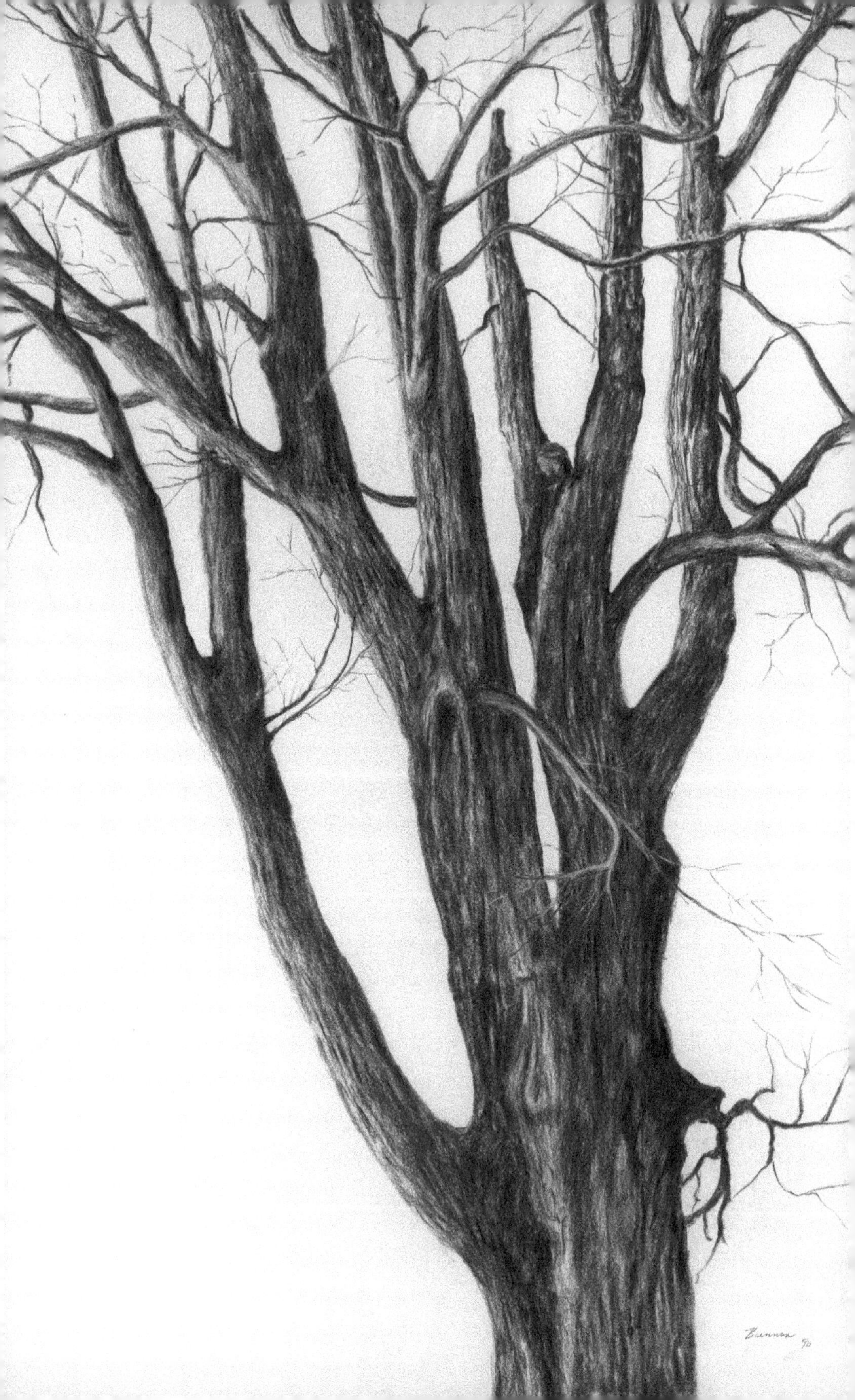

Brennan
90

Recognizing that some structural order is needed, I have chosen the one that is the most dependable and familiar of all: chance, pure, unadulterated chance. Arbitrariness follows. The fact that it is totally arbitrary, in this case, is something that we all will have to live with; however, in a special irony, although the actual content of the work is arranged arbitrarily, the pages of the book are more or less in alphabetical order. Go figure. Here is the ultimate orderliness, sparring with ambiguity. Like a challenge? Read on.

It is my hope that as the reader turns each page, a new experience will be found, perhaps, familiar, perhaps, not.

ROBERT BRENNAN

Come Sit with Me

Come sit with me on my deck.
If you look long enough,
you will see the trees darken in the setting sun.
Having just lost their leaves,
they stand as bare as your thoughts and mine.
Visible is all that had been hidden by the grand opera
of greens of all tones and shades and values.
Emerges that house out back,
lit by the setting sun,
all bright greys and whites of the trim
whose image is broken up by statuesque trunks and branches,
standing now in the early November light,
and promising in their very carriage
that they will survive the winter
that waits around some undefined corner.

The sky is the most beautiful cerulean,
with contrails streaming from south to north
as testament that some pilgrim-loaded jet
has passed by on its way from JFK or LaGuardia,
headed up across the Connecticut countryside,
and toward the New England Coast,
over Cape Cod or Maine,
out over the North Atlantic to romantic Paris
or Rome
or London.

Come sit with me,
as the reflections bypassed in daily living emerge
as the breeze slows
and the sun starts its descent
and the sparrow,
perched on the highest branch,
surveys his prospects for a resting place for the night,
and you and I,
in a rare moment,
watch,
as he flies off.
The air cools.
We gather our dishes and glasses and cups
and move inside.

A Modest Wish

If a soul be granted a lifelong wish
of knowing how and why
he bears the common anguish
of those who turned out shy,

still, it is more like turning in,
like hiding under many covers,
living beneath lonely skin,
hoping for friendly lovers.

Crossing rooms of judging eyes
is surely in the walker's head,
yet no less real are these lies
that the shy have learned to dread.

In truth, there is no cage
from which the soul must flee.
All the world is not a stage
wherein all notice thee.

The meek might inherit the earth,
yet it seems unlikely to me.
'Tis best to accept one's worth
and to live fiercely free.

A Nauset Memory

When upon the deep, dark, endless beach,
the silver waves break,
lighted by a silent moon
and stars that float in the melodies of the night,
all gathered in configurations of fantasy
and imagining of gods and goddesses
and hunters and the hunted,
and the comet,
whose brilliant tail makes its diagonal crossing of the blue-black night,
inspiring "Ahs!" in the young and in the old.
Here in this primordial place,
jutting into the sea,
miles away from skies muted by the lights of human progress,
tracks left in sands, still warm after the setting of the sun,
lose their edges to the gentle sea breeze.
And except for the sound of crashing waves
in this cathedral of the earth and of the sky and of the sea,
there is silence.
In this cathedral of the inspired heart, there is awe.
In this awakened knowledge of the splendor of the earth,
there is hope.

A New Music

There will come a day when
melodies will fill the air,
floating down from ceilings
and up from floors,
from open doors and windows,
from behind walls,
melodies that will float over seas
and move the souls of those
speaking different tongues,
melodies as language,
sounds set in meter and rhythm
or long, straight, and curving lines
that resonate off acoustical walls
or trees or stars on a moonlit night.

The voice, as well, may carry across space
the colors and shapes of nature first
and then the minds of men,
all formed in images that require magic to exist,
or the dance of the human body
and the dance of words across the page
and across the sea
that will move the hearts of the young
and the old of every nation.

There will come a day
when the great treasure of steel,
invested in rifles and tanks will be melted
and recast as bridges and sculptures,
and young men across the globe, united, will
refuse to march or aim a weapon at one of their own.

For the earth to survive, much must be sacrificed,
beginning with the loss of WE and THEM
and the birth of US.
Let the music celebrate this new beginning
and hope for salvation of planet Earth.

A Transport of the Soul

Is Sunny Ridge Road from west to east or east to west?
Navigation is enhanced
by views as splendid
as those from a country road in Vermont,
rolling fields of yellow-green grass with bluebells
and rhododendron and the occasional mountain laurel,
and in the distance,
the young crop of blue spruce, hemlocks, and white pines add their
repetitive triangles
in the process of growing up into someone's Christmas tree.
And crisscrossing and surrounding all are walls of stones,
stacked one upon the other, six to eight stones high,
winding their way around the perimeter of the land
as they did a century ago,
all shades of grey and umber and burnt sienna, and some, whitish,
formed from the bleaching of the sun.

Standing in the space it had claimed before the building of the walls
and the laying down of the black top road,
a row of stately sugar maples informs the historical imagination.
Some have weathered the drying heat of summer
and the bitter cold and the snows of a Connecticut winter,
with only minor damage.
Others have lost branches and struggle to keep from the further
splitting of trunks
and rotting of listlessly hanging branches.
And moving slowly in the summer's heat, oxen find nourishment in the
thick, green grass
and solitude in a gentle breeze beneath the shadows of the maple.

And at day's end, the slow ritual,
learned through years of the repetitive trek from barn to field
and back again
in the oppressive heat of summer
and again during autumn's change from green to yellows and reds
and oranges and violets,
all standing against a sky transitioning from cerulean to cobalt
to deep purple
as the wind guides the leaves of the maple in a swirl across the open field
to find their final resting places up against stone walls
and on the leeward side of hills in the gullies.
There is implicit in all the history of the farmer the planting of things
that grow,
guiding oxen to the barn from their youth,
setting evergreens to grow straight.
Buried in his DNA, the love of the land grows
as men find their cause of taking what the land has to offer
and giving back as good custodians,
the way of the farmer,
passed from father to son.

A Rightful Debt

I know the debt that's owed the Frost.
Whom he owes, I dare not say.
It was then of another day.
Without forebears, we all are lost.

Brick upon brick, build the wall.
Solid foundations avoid the fall.
Being square where rectangles rule
is the way of genius or of fool.

The living cannot erase the ghost,
nor offer tin words or empty toast.
What seems so brilliant in your text
echoes from another's breast

of long ago, of another land
of another's mind and mentor's hand.
You walk by garden's gate
with winter as your fate.

You dare not write of mending fences,
but know of such things in your senses.
The smell of decaying leaf
belongs to you, not as thief,

but as a kindred spirit, humbled
by footsteps large and deep,
buried in the clay you hope
to reshape before you sleep.

A Warmer Wind

It is spring,
and I will ride through the countryside
beneath branches spreading across the road
with buds about to burst.
I will open the moon roof
to allow warm winds to enter the cabin and my soul.
Around the twists and turns of country roads,
through Poverty Hollow,
an Eden of expansive farm lands and waterfalls on the edge of ponds,
sitting quietly, reflecting a world beneath the sun.
Oh, how we tried to find that brilliant trout
who managed to outwit us year after year,
when I was younger, and both of my knees worked.
This day, bridging the end of winter
and the long-awaited return of Spring,
air of warm moisture and hopefulness,
rises with welcoming hearts.
And all along the edges of the world,
in forests and along the broad, expansive horizon
beyond the beach and ocean,
all awaiting the time of the reawakening.
This old man blasts the melodies on his radio through the roof
as the sounds of "Hound Dog" and Elvis rise again,
if only in my ears of reverential memory.
Around corners, tightly, wheels squealing,
short and long hairs flowing in the breeze
as in the early days,
when floating above roads on 32psi raised the spirit,
making, for the time, all things right with the world.
It can be that way again, you know,
with judicious use of cruise control, that is.
Ah, sweet shade beneath the maples.

American Diamond

All across the land, diamonds sparkle in the sun,
all greens and off-red tan,
and lines that drive to waiting gloves,
Gonzales to Cohen, and back to McDuff.
Without words, this sacred pact:
"We are in this together."
Free-flowing scoop, handoff, and whip it,
short to second, to first,
each with a passionate thirst
for winning.

Each star upon this stage
is lit by a trusting heart.
This covenant shall not be split apart,
that each will be as one,
yet none will stand alone,
that each will make his mark
on the diamond's brilliant spark.

All across this land,
on manicured, green-acre fields,
on ragged, hard-packed sand,
no goal could be more grand
to those upon the field
or the faithful in the stand,
that the valiant shall never yield,

that for each in mortal battle,
character shall be revealed.

All across this land,
diamonds sparkle in the sun.

Back to School

O, troubled heart, youth's loss of freedom in the woods.

O, aching heart, at slipping away, long days, warm ocean breezes,
and concerts on the green.

O, breaking heart, at the loss of dreams conjured in early spring
or in the depths of winter.

Fireflies and constellations, stars in free fall or staying still, provide
illumination for the darkened soul.

Stick ball and kick-the-can end as street lights sputter to life
for the return home.

O, troubled heart, youth's loss of freedom on the beach.

O, aching heart, at the counting of remaining days.

O, breaking heart, yearning to relive spent days of searing sunlight,
rejects the consolation of clear, cool, autumnal air.

First sting of Fall descends in transitional days,
and nights that leave behind a crystal dew.

Dressed in new, bright pouches on their backs,
youths line back roads and city streets.

Yellow dragons collect their prey at designated stops along the way.

Smiling, greeting faces gather at the gate, no doubt, meaning well
to welcome visitors to temporary Hell.

All is not lost, for those who pass o'er many bars
gain wisdom to heal the scars.

Aspiring Together

I know.
I'll be Jesus Christ.
You'll be the Virgin Mary.
Of course, we both know that these two parts have been taken,
but, perhaps, in the off-Broadway version or the off-off-Broadway version,
I will be Jesus Christ.
You will be the Virgin Mary.
We will fashion our scenes and actions after the originals,
having studied their every move.
The essence of our parts will migrate
from our brains and our hearts
down into the depths of our souls.
We will spend each moment of our day,
when we are conscious,
striving for perfection.
We will spend each night behind the veil of sleep,
conjuring up ever new ways to improve the faulty performance
of our last show.
You will be my supporting actor.
I will support you as well.
We will take our show on the road,
playing Tulsa, Oklahoma or Bangor, Maine.
We will, at all times, act as surrogates for each other,
offering helpful criticisms.
Wherever we play, we will strive for Broadway quality performances.
When you fail, I will lift you up.

When I fail, you will buy me pizza and beer,
and after our failing performances,
we will sit together in a cozy bistro in Paduka,
or Buffalo,
or Roanoke, Virginia.
We will kiss away each other's tears.
In time, perhaps, we will recognize
that despite our imperfections,
we were loved by our audiences,
even in Seattle.

Aunt Frances I

Welcomed always at the White Way Theatre,
each day, Francis walks along Davenport, quietly, slightly stooped over.
Concerns, discarded at the door, leave room
for coming attractions, the dancing of Astaire and Rogers,
torrid love affairs, staring Ava Gardner with some bigger-than-life guy,
and then Micky Mouse,
as well as news of bombs,
bursting in Africa or in France,
with German, French, American, and English young men,
all trying to kill "the enemy,"
all reflected in the somber News of the Day,
cast upon the screen,
40x50 feet in broad black and white,
and, later, colored visions of madness,
far beyond the Great White Way and Davenport Avenue.

There is a brief turn to reality:
that one in the family, so loved, has been sent off,
from this earth,
in the madness of Nazi and American tank forces in Africa.
What is there to do with sadness,
the kind that hurts for young souls sent to their graves by old men,
hoping to revive their masculinity in the name of protecting their country?

Aunt Francis, diabetes and all,
seeking truth through stories of real life, different from hers,
cast her beliefs and truth in the darkness,
lit only in that rectangle of light, way up forward,

projecting visions of a world, real and imagined,
filling the emptiness of whatever was absent
in the third-floor tenement.

There appears nothing that will impede the walk of Aunt Francis
up Davenport Avenue to the Great White Way Theatre.
The truth circulates around and above this world,
but is true only to the truth of the one living in the back row, aisle seat
of the Great White Way Theatre.

Beating Around the Language

Some poems are so obtuse,
they make of a red chicken
a bright white goose.
"Chickens are not red," you say.
"Well, they were in my day."
Why should credulity come into play?
It is all a fantasy, you know,
this using words so pictures show.
"Your words have double meanings,"
she complains.
"Yes," he confirms," and with great pains,
I wrote, 'You are my sunshine,'
but meant,
'You are round with golden hair.'"
"Do you think," says she, "that this is fair?"
"I must first assess what makes the critics care,"
says he.
"I must write words that truly flow,
like in the flight of the winter crow.
As I have learned in poetry school,
there is a rule,
you know, about calling a crow a crow.
There are better ways to describe a winter crow:
black oval form, riding zephyrs and gusts,
floating above white blanket, casting below
Payne's grey echo, rising and falling,
leaving behind a memory of flight.

"What of clarity?" says she. "As in,
'The black crow casts its shadow on the white snow
as it flies over the landscape.'"
"Well," says he,
"What do you want at night,
the facts or a fantastical flight,
poetry or news of the day?"
Confuse the two, and there will be hell to pay.

Before the Revolution

In the early days, long before the Revolution,
there was the gathering of the stones,
the stretching of the bones,
always for just cause,
on sleds fashioned by genius,
hewn of oak and ash,
waxed to glide upon paths of hardened ice and knee-deep snow,
tasks each boy would come to know,
trees made tall and stout by time,
reshaped as humble homes set in rhyme
on the edge of growing fields
spread across the landscape,
a new world promising survival for the prepared
and extinction for the presumptuous.
Walls abound with foundations deep beneath the frost line,
one side holding in the dreams of a brave, new frontier,
the other holding out the despot's agents,
who threaten with muskets to breach the walls of free men
who have traded the fear of the monarchy
for the hope of a government conceived by the governed.
Stone walls do not a fortress make but line the claim of the Patriot's stand,
where he builds his home and begets sons and daughters
and beliefs in the rightness of freedom
and the inherent dignity of all men,
a world where the only monarchs left
fly across the fields of corn
and land on garden flowers.

Behind the Clouds

Muffled sounds, heading east,
trailing off, a turn northward,
lost in blue and white clouds,
floating as mist,
soft edges,
no lines to be found between the blue and the white.
What sweet sounds below: the singing of a mother,
melodious and heart lifting,
preparing for the sun to set
and for the moon to rise.
What instinct follows here,
the treasure found in searching
the wonder of the sparrow's daily song
and feeding time at dusk.

Belief

You can believe in green.
There are others who believe in red.
It doesn't really matter.
I knew a guy who believed in orange.
He married a girl who believed in blue.
It was a constant battle,
but on rare occasions,
they brought out the best in each other.
Mary Grey said that it was all bullshit.
"What you believe," she said, "is all in your head.
Just relax.
Nobody's beliefs are better nor worse than any others,
and nobody really cares anyway.
Trust me. I have seen it from every angle.
Everybody wants to stand out.
To get them to understand that no one is better than another is impossible.
Some guy comes along and says,
'Everybody is always changing anyway,
and who they are depends on whom they are standing next to
or in front of.
Imagine.'
So, everybody is so damn fickle.
I would call them all chameleons,
but, hey,
it is no threat to my black ass.
Let them believe whatever they want."

Blankets

Sleep does not erase the mortal story
that awakens with the morning glory,
muttering from the other side,
fits of twist, roller coaster ride,

buried 'neath a grand veneer,
myths and truths to fear,
floating about in starless skies
between God and the devil's eyes.

Beneath the pain and muffled cries,
tears flowing from sad goodbyes,
words on stone, words so kind
for the still awake, left behind.

Oh, memories, claim your place.
Within this maelstrom space,
tragedy be replaced with love,
rejoining souls from below
and from above.

Bitter

Bitter, biting breeze,
enough to make a freeze,
diamonds in the trees,

darkened clouds,
flowers in shrouds,
birds huddled in crowds.

Between fall and spring,
nightingales still sing.
All must cling
to belief in the winter sun
when snows have begun,
and adjustments are done.

Bitter, biting cold,
snapping at the old.

More stories to be told
around the fireplace,
lighting every face,
tales of courage and grace.

When I was young,
songs of winter were sung
as we trod off to school,
one by one.

That's when snow was really deep,
and we had promises to keep.
There was no time to sleep.

We were told,
"What you sow, you will reap."
That's when I was young,
and did I mention,
the snow was really deep.

Blooming Cares

Do not bloom in my mind, you little care,
like a balloon taking in air.
Keep your place in line,
and all will be fine,
not fine as in
"Go away!"
nor to save the day,
but to stop mind chatter
that loses sight
of what should matter.
Consider,
as you curse your cane,
those in far greater pain.

Blue Eyes

Blue eyes,
cast down,
almost always.
China blue eyes,
wet eyes,
reflecting sparkles of light,
aided by Hulls brew.
Tissues,
folded many times,
blocked tear ducts
and sadness,
the long, quiet kind,
learned over years
through events that bend backs.
Low esteem,
believed for too long,
from childhood
through child birth,
through sandstorms,
and rogue waves
and floors that shift beneath the feet.
Knees with reason to tremble
stand upright,
supported by character,
driven by courage
found in circumstance.
China blue eyes smile
at modest, favorable winds.

Boat Yard Bird

Boat Yard Bird builds his nest in the welcoming hole
at the end of the boom of the dormant C&C.
What better perch for an old bird
who knows his way around the boatyard?
There he sits, then flits away
to capture discarded French fries,
thrown by filled-up kids
from the deck of the boat yard restaurant.
What more could an old boat yard bird want
this eighteenth day of May in the year 2019?
Perhaps, what most old boat yard birds want,
a bigger boat, new sails, a sunny spring,
a winter home in Florida,
enough worms in the nest to take the day off.
Some things are serendipitous.
What bird would have thought that Sparkman and Stevens
had left a nesting hole in the boom
of one of their greatest designs?
There must be another explanation.
Who would have thought
that so many captains of spring boats still on the hard
must push aside their grey hair
and favor their arthritic knees
as they ascend and descend their ladders?
What richness of dreams sits upon winter stands?

When nesting is done,
this bird and whoever follows
will take flight out over the channel,
alighting in the branches of trees,
home to birds of every shape, color, and persuasion,
even those whose earliest days were spent
inside the boom of a C&C sailing yacht.
Other old birds will be cast off from the launching well
and will head out,
amid feelings of anxiety and excitement,
the stuff of which every voyage is made.

Blue Bird Sings and Dances

This refrain:
if only I could dance,
my career
would have a chance.
The world would be
my stage,
not this silly branch.
Grateful for my splendid voice,
I long for another choice.
If I had my way,
I would shuffle off to Broadway.
Enough of Pavarotti.
I, too, can hit high C.
Who will hear it
atop this nowhere tree?
Light up my beak and wing.
I will make the rafters ring.
There is a story, they say,
of a tapdancing blue jay,
who, from an early age,
longed for any stage,
and,
despite his mother's rage,
who might have put him in a cage,
he abandoned Law and Primary Care
and auditioned for a part

One would think that just this rarity,
which had no parity,
would gain him much love
as he tapdanced above
the head of the crowd,
but they were so loud,
the rhythmic beat of his feet
was never heard.
Now, don't you think it appeared absurd,
a crazy, wiggly bird
jumping around on a wire
as if his pants were on fire?
Oh, and every act at that county fair
had a costume it had to wear,
dancing blue jays, most of all.
Somehow, it made him look so tall.
Sadly,
dancing on a wire can make one tire.
Our exhausted blue jay had a fateful fall.
Now blue jay flies above the tent,
curving and carving through the sky,
capturing every young child's eye,
following his natural bent
and, all in all, feeling quite content.

California Burning

Lower Manhattan turning
back to the sea.
Yellow jackets swarming
out of anger,
stinging, warning.
Hearts gone cold
dig for gold.
Footprints, once in rich, moist earth
now raise dust,
carried by winds
singing mournful songs
through trees, bent
like the backs of old men.
Eagles fly on high,
seeking a quiet sky
beyond the crackling
of the pines,
beyond the sound of sinking glass and stone,
monuments to forever,
beyond the silence of denial, beyond the sky,
where there are no cartographic lines separating countries,
simply shades of grey in tones warm and cool, rising in what was day
and in the night chromatic black,
blacks mixed from the altered alchemy of the light, new formulations.
Dark air, pushed by dark winds, unforgiving winds,
Chaos,
created by the genius
and arrogance
of mankind.

Bully's Search

Oh, I can find your fatal sin.
Perhaps, you are too fat or maybe too thin.
And, then again, it could be
the color of your skin.
I have always liked a nice, milky hue.
If it's good enough for me,
it is certainly good enough for you.
Do not doubt what I can find
when at my most unkind.
Any quality that I deem rare:
too big ears and scruffy hair.
I once found six fingers on just one hand.
Oh, that was just so wonderfully grand.
When my skills are challenged as a mystery,
I answer with reference to history,
a treasure trove of ethnic slurs,
found in the most colorful words,
describing those of the bully's choice,
spoken in a hateful voice,
or sometimes in a velvet tone,
or with a touch of levity,
while cutting to the bone,
long tested words of brevity —
"Kike," "Harp," "Spic," or "Kraut" —
labels the bigot may write or whisper or shout
on the playground or in a note,
circulating about,
or from the Despot's lectern
in speeches meant to burn
and shatter glass,
advocating for one perfect class.

Cellist of Kharkiv

The scream of air raid sirens
bite the human ear,
bring terror to the human heart.
Still,
the melodies of Bach
bring peace to the human soul in the square,
amid bombed-out buildings,
homes of young men and women
and old men and old women,
of children, of pets, dogs and cats,
and multiplying gerbils, studied by little boys,
and plants from seed, a school project about life
and taking care of things that grow,
studied by little girls in little pots on sun-filled window sills.
And in the square,
between the bombing times,
the young cellist and Bach,
beyond all bombings and brutality,
the coming and going of murderous despots,
the building and leveling of armies,
sits upon a simple folding chair,
placed in the bombed-out square.
The sole cellist prevails,
and the melodies of Bach
rise upon zephyrs of acrid air into the same blue sky
that has floated over man's brilliant mind
and corrupt soul for centuries,
and from a single heart,

hands that guide the bow across the strings
and bring into the air melodies of hope,
even as embers smoke.
When they have burned out,
it is the melodies of Bach,
played courageously in the ravaged village square
which shall do what they have done for centuries,
set peace and beauty and humanism afloat above the battlefield,
beyond hate.

Camouflage

Do not paint wood that has rotted away
on a fence destined to stay
only until its final day.
Like perfume placed upon trash
or ointment upon a painful rash,
in the desert a mirage,
in the jungle camouflage,
from the minds of crooked men,
black venom from their pen,
again and again and again,
and from their mouths a curse,
repeated verse after verse after verse,
placing truth within its hearse.
Do not paint wood that has rotted away.
Do not let corrupted souls
rule the day.

Childhood Dream

When the childhood dream warps and shatters,
and the dreamer confronts what matters,
in the wake, avoid the shards
of scattered hopes not in the cards.
In time, through ever-changing eyes
that weather ever-changing skies,
new paths, never before seen,
emerge amid the parting of the green.
Hills, once thought too tall to climb,
dreams, once thought too big to dream,
change in scale of a different kind,
living now in a changing mind.

Which hopeful soul does not lament
youthful dreams' sad descent?
"Follow your dreams," the sage will say.
"Do not forget to honor play,
as the weight of living every day
threatens to steal all dreams away."
'Tis best that dreams deepen in time,
that the dreamer writes a new rhyme.
While some words will rightly change,
some will merely rearrange.
No story of dreams is complete half way through.
Every twist and turn exposes what is true,
that when every dream has been spent,
those thought to be broken were only bent.

Caressing the Truth

The hopefuls speak
this exhausted prayer:
"The truth shall set us free."

Wise guys in snake skin
know in their hearts
the truth will lock them up.

In the old days, when truth was true,
men knew when they had lied
before all facts turned grey.

Righteous witnesses could say,
"This is what it is."
All in the circle could see.

In the new days, those so inclined
have traded the gift of Sight
for the blindness of Ignorance,
eyes and ears closed tight,
taking the coward's stance
while the bully picked the fight.

None dare take a final glance
at Credulity's final flight
in its sad, deathly dance
in the darkness of the night.

In the old days, when the truth was true,
lying leaders of men
who breached the sacred code
again and again and again,
exposing absence of character,
were directed to the crooked road,

leading to another place,
where the truth did not matter,
nor were lies a disgrace.
Those gathered around the bully in the ring,
whose face had turned liars red,
finally felt the mortal sting
of where their hearts and minds had led.

In the new days, the kissing of the bully's ring
makes the weak feel strong, the frightened safe,
erasing lines between right and wrong
to secure their space in a truth-forsaken place.

Children in the Yard

When baseball is the game,
and the sun, low in the sky,
promises two more hours,
and in our hearts the anticipation
of yards full of flowers,
grown all but in the diamond
where young feet have raced
from first to home,
one step after another, carefully placed,
this shall be home as history,
and a bare spot declares,
"And first shall be the gate,
and second,
evenly spaced by the naked eye,
will be mid-lawn,
and the hedge shall be third.
Home shall be a path of hurrahs
and teases and taunts
and chests stuck out,
a nearly straight line,
no more than twenty feet,
where the young have run,
brother after brother,
cousin after cousin,
year after year,
Easter after Easter,
spring after spring,
forming alliances of love,
alliances of family,
that will meet in the springtime sun,
when all the world is met with sadness for the missing
and hope that this diamond is forever.

Chimes

Sweet sounds of chimes
soften winter's crimes,
moving with the wind
in deep, melancholy tones,
bringing to branches,
darkened with sorrow,
the voice of hope.
And across the yard,
the soprano cousin,
answering the tenor baritone and bass,
sounds gentle as two feathers
touching in the wind,
small metal tubes releasing
voices waiting to touch the hearts
of those who pass by.
Even as the first flakes fall,
the wind sets in motion
the first symphony of the winter.
Sweet sounds of chimes
soften winter's crimes.

Clearing Out

Errant words I just erase
and watch fly off the page.
Things are yet another case,
serving as the owner's cage
and claiming all visible space.
Would that I could erase
the detritus of an earlier age
without regret nor feeling loss.
Empty boxes, saved for the return,
I would cut up or brightly burn,
or, into recycling sprightly toss
corrugations of all kind,
vowing to only leave behind
a gem to which I had been blind.
A floor and open air
within now-visible walls appear.
So, each spring, when duty calls,
and the sun is warm,
and the grass has grown,
I face the chaos with a moan.
No, winter is a better time
to rectify this age-old crime.
This is a time to be outdoors,
not to do these hateful chores.

As I deign to ponder options all,
it occurs to me there is the Fall,
with its clean, crisp air, and I
with energy to spare,
I choose then what I must,
the final days of August,
and, if I remember,
continue on through September.
I have not begun, but the plan is set.
'Tis time to remove my thinking cap,
to settle in for a well-earned nap.

Comfort Food

So, when you're old and can't roller skate anymore,
and your chances at water skiing have dried up,
and you can't bowl, even with those little duck pin balls,
and you think that everything is all over,
and you think, "What is left?"
Well, here is what is left: Italian food:
parmigiana, mozzarella, lasagna al forno, pizza, pasta fagioli,
sauce, sauce, sauce,
sauce with basil, sauce with cheese, sauce with oregano,
a world of reds and greens, swirling in a pot,
and fat men and ladies, sitting at the table as round as their bellies,
all laughing over some funny memories,
over sausage and peppers,
while young people, looking on, wonder,
"What is so funny?
You are old. How can you laugh like that?"
"Fettuccini," I say to them.
"If you do not know fettuccini, you are young and uninformed
and, probably, dumb."
Comfort food, Fool.
Life is about comfort food.
Oh, sure, one has to grow into it, but after roller skating,
you only count the years until comfort food is your life.

Take pictures of what you bake. Send them out to your followers:
sausage and pepper grinders parmigiana. Heaven!
"You will see," says the little old lady with brilliant, silver-gray hair,
a black shawl covering her shoulders.
After duck pin bowling and mass every morning,
candles lit for the souls of the departed,
life is Italian food: eggplant parmigiana, veal beneath the cheese,
laughter over broken bread dipped in olive oil.
You love your wife, and bring pasta to her bedside
after the roller skating and the water skiing and the wrestling in bed.
Comfort! Ah, comfort is whole and round and pulled from the oven
and cut into triangles of bubbling hot mozzarella, tomatoes,
and toppings of your choice.
What is it they say:
"To go or to stay?"
I say, "Stay,
at least another day.
The cannoli are on the way."

Commencement

All applaud for my beloved, standing in line,
awaiting the procession of youth dressed as penguins,
with square hats facing the light of the stage,
the affirmation of goals achieved,
journey to end,
journey to begin.
I will applaud for the diamond of your heart,
seated in the row across from the diamond of my heart.
Our voices will form a duet.
Others will join.
We will have a trio and then a chorus
when, in unison, they walk toward the light,
and upon passing through,
will make of our once scraped knees,
self-doubting, self-assured, unconfident, confident.
Hopeful loved one, seated in row 75,
in the college of his passion,
waiting their turn to go off into the world,
changed in the most profound way.
There will be no change in height or weight or color of the hair,
but beginning on the inside,
working the magic of the self to become.
And you and I, witnesses from places far and near,
witnesses who bring the dialects and accents and colors of America,
cheer for each other's loved ones,
without knowledge of names,
save for those called out in pride,
and dream fulfilled tears.

"Ava! Ava! Evan! Evan! Alonzo! Alonzo!"
And the air, carrying the melodies of the ages,
Pomp and Circumstance
and flourishes of the music of kings and queens fills the space,
floats above the heads and into the rafters,
surrounding the young souls walking,
those who have been nurtured and loved.
In unison, tassels are shifted from left to right,
caps are sent off into space as balloons fall from above.
Profound is the change in the world

Covering Things

The Lichen glows green against the host
that stands tall and black mid fading light,
as days lose their edge against the night.

Living things of all description that once in sunlight
stood against the green gone over to ochre,
now rest in stacks of silence,

waiting for the coat that will hide them from the wind,
that will make a darkened space
beneath a skin formed by the snow.

And implements of the yard are gathered.
Watering hoses, lying snakelike, are coiled.
Benches, darkened by weather, are draped.

Storm windows change places with screens.
All manner of drafts are sought out.
Mousetraps are counted and readied for use.

Critters, two foot and four, who once found comfort outside,
prepare for the journey inside the walls, under the roof,
pulling around themselves wraps that protect,

making for themselves nests that warm,
gathering up all things in preparation for shorter days,
climbing beneath the blankets to hear pelting on the roof,

dimming the lights at dusk to watch, in silence, white flakes,
guided by zephyrs, that fall in such abundance that the land,
once pock-marked, becomes harmonious.

All things, moving and not moving, covered, tucked away.

Compass Heading

No sailor dare curse the wind,
Nor voyager a favorable tide.
No wise fisherman leaves pole untended,
nor nets unmended,
nor anchor rode untied.

Guardian of the garden's promise
takes not for granted spring rain,
nor the richness of the soil,
nor the weathered muscles' pain,
nor the hours of toil,
swelling every vein.

Every being on the earth,
mollusk to man,
has instinct from birth
and bound by the plan
There for the taking
and whenever he can
Of his own making

Stirring the philosopher's plea,
the pot in which questions bubble,
to what degree is man free
to invent his own trouble?

No sailor dare curse the wind,
nor voyager a favorable tide,
but if he must sail a certain track,
he would be wise to learn to tack.

Contrasts

I did not start this way,
thinking that words were of the night or of the day.
I only wanted to say what I thought there was to say.
In time, it was the human race
that filled the empty space
upon my page,
all forms of kindness and rage,
just as others, wanting to see
how it was meant to be,
what had been foretold
so difficult to hold,
stories of the meek,
stories of the bold,
seekers of love,
spreaders of hate,
and those who step between
two fires burning bright,
each believing their righteous fight
will rid the world of night.
What man can show his face,
believing the world would be a better place
if he could just erase
this one race?
There is no need to look around.
He has been found
in every time,
in every land,
among cultures modest and grand.

What fissure lies within the human heart
that it can be pulled apart
by the rantings of a fool,
using fear, his favorite tool?
"What will you lose?" is the bigot's call.
"They will cause you to lose it all.
Far too much brightness you have made
to slide beneath the other's shade.
The moon and stars were made for you," he claims.
"As for the sun? Yes, that, too.
Who comes to take it all away
in the darkest night,
in the brightest day?
And who," the bigot asks, "is ready for the fight?"
It did not start this way,
thinking words were of the night or of the day.
The good man, withholding words he needs to say,
enables the bigot's play
and promises another darkened day

Cruising

How joyful it was, heading east on an outgoing tide,
passing Stratford Point and the waters off Milford Harbor,
the early morning wind,
struggling to strengthen its push from the southwest,
and the steel jib,
chugging away in concert with the raised main,
as quiet as its very nature would allow,
passing the New Haven breakwater,
feeling the push of the current,
and we, in its spell,
thinking our superb sailing was pushing us along.

And beyond, my beloved Momauguin Beach,
where I once sat at water's edge
and watched, along the horizon, great sailing vessels,
heading west or heading east, as I was now doing.
I had become the stuff of my memories.
I had become the stuff of my never-imagined-to-be-realized dreams.

As a scruffy twelve-year-old, I sat upon Happy Fenton's Beach,
with my feet cooling in the waters of Long Island Sound,
gazing out at the elegant sails moving ever so slowly across the horizon,
against skies made more brilliantly blue in recall,
memories of other days in Mansfield Grove,
sitting on the work bench with some friends,
listening to the tales of Charlie Bartlet, master boat builder,
tell of how he built the rum runners, back in the twenties,
that ran "hootch" up from someplace in New Jersey
to a rendezvous off the Long Island Coast
and then into Connecticut to the gin mills of New Haven and elsewhere.
With every stroke of his plane,

Charlie's skill at shaping cedar and oak
into the most graceful rowboats became apparent,
rowboats for hire to weekend fishermen from New Haven.

And I, at eleven or twelve, along with friends,
cleaned out the returned rentals of empty worm and beer cans,
crumbled newspaper left over from fish wrapping,
and all the other detritus that had been left behind,
and then the final bailing out and tying up to the mooring stake,
using the finally-mastered clove hitch, taught to us by some older kid,
or, maybe even, Charlie himself.

It was in these very waters, that years back,
in one of Charlie's twelve-footers,
my buddy and I fashioned a makeshift sail on a sapling mast and boom
and rowed along Momauguin Beach until, with boom out,
we caught the prevailing southwesterly breeze
and headed out past the Farm River entrance and Kelsey's Island,
past the rock outcroppings at Short Beach,
and just to the edge of the entrance to the Branford River.
And then, depending upon the time of day and the friendliness of the waves,
debated the wisdom of continuing on to the Thimble Islands,
where we might uncover the buried treasure of Captain Cook,
or with a sun lower in the western sky and waves beginning to kick up,
we came about, leaving the adventure east for another day,
which came, in fact,
many times, throughout the spring and summer of our twelfth year
upon this earth,
emerging each time down the Farm River, over to Bobby's house,
just off the beach,
to pick up our sailing gear and head eastward.

Delayed Response

Wait too long; the words are gone.
Yet,
they may return as would any song
that arises from a living place,
silent for so long,
not written on the face,
but in a lower place,
where ideas belong,
gifts for the human race.
The poet must believe
that in life's unending squeeze,
spillings from the heart and mind
float on every wistful breeze
that the soul of the searcher hopes to find.
Still, there is a cost
when what is lost
was more true than what is found.
Some say it is all in the sound.
What flows as from an unblocked stream
that flows so from the heart
as feather or as hammer,
elegant words or halting stammer,
is where the poetry must start.

Dream Dance

Dance with me in my dream.
As for me, I will flow around the floor as if my shoes were riding on air,
and you, not needing the emancipation of a dream,
will, as always, float as if your body and soul were composed of sound,
rhythms that make a lover's leap into the mix of unseeable airwaves,
alive in magic, emitting colors and tones of warmth and coldness,
sounds emerging from horns and strings and drums,
all emerging from souls dancing through melodies
to be gathered up in the heart as they pass by.
Dance with me in my dreams.
For me, it will be as if no one is watching,
save for the only heart I trust to witness my stumbles.
Yet, here is the magic I promise in my dreams.
My feet will move with the rhythm of my soul,
carefree, foregoing thoughts of self and feet of concrete,
but on the floor, all gleaming in polished hardwood splendor,
wide and round, a space for just we two.
I will hold you,
and our feet and our loving hearts, and our souls,
promised to our shared melody, will soar.
Dance with me in my dreams.

Despot's Dream

I have a dream
that my children will grow up in a country
where they are judged,
not by the content of their character,
but by the color of their skin
and the cut of their clothing.

I have a dream
that the sons of bankers
and the sons of moguls
will study together in schools
for the better people of society,
far away from the darker side
of this world.

I have a dream
that across this great land,
from the dark and dank air of Seattle,
to the suffocating heat of Miami,
our youth will learn the most enduring values
that our fathers and grandfathers
have passed on to us.
Win at any cost; cunning outtrumps
blind adherence to outdated rules,
designed for suckers.

I have a dream
that my sons will have
the great opportunity for happiness

that can be found
through loving a special woman,
as well as others, special for the moment.

I have a dream
that the air of our great country,
from the Blue Ridge Mountains of West Virginia,
to the whitest mountains of New Hampshire,
will be filled with the billowing smoke
of rekindled progress, dug out of our ancestral grounds,
deep beneath the earth and the lungs of heroic men,
directed by the pens of greedy men, floors above,
who share jeers from lines of the unclean
as they drive past them on the way home
in their Bentleys.

I have a dream
that men, living high in their exclusive aeries above New York City,
when it floods,
will tie their yachts to railings
of sixth floor balconies,
and I will tie my yacht to my tower
and my hopes to the manly gain of gold.

I vow to push my way ahead of the rest.
My rich friends and I will all get there.
We will get to the promised land,
so help me, Lucifer

Duck

I know no duck
from Peking,
New York, nor LA
who would say.
"Let me be your entertainment.
Let me show the way.
Once warmed by your fateful fire,
you should not tire
from twisting my spindly legs,
which will inspire
taste buds to come to life,
erasing weekly strife."

With some remorse, I say,
"All souls have their day,
some to take and some to take away."
In all I do, my heart is true.
For a short time, I lament
that in the food chain, you,
with all your charms well spent,
sit in glory upon this table.
I know you are a duck,
but what a glorious duck you are.
We have admired you from afar,
but tonight, we wash our hands of criminal intent.
We mean no harm,
but as pigs and cows and chicks testify:
"It does no good to cry.
People are going to eat you."

Ebony

Ebony, mahogany, or knotty pine?
As for me,
knotty pine is fine.
It is of the softer woods, you know.
When six feet under,
safe against the drying sun and freezing snow,
it is still in pine's nature to rot away to dust
as has been promised in the scriptures.
That's all right with me.
Mahogany and ebony
have always been beyond
my hopes for the future.
Perhaps, there is in the hard woods
something of lasting substance,
but in the end, not for me.
Cast not your money to the past
but toward the future,
where it must last.

Eastern Savings Time

A Connecticut Yankee
throws nothing away.
He saves all from an earlier day.
His wife tells him right to his face,
"Look, you have stolen all of our space.
Here, this box of left over string,
what good could that truly bring?"
So now it is another spring.
"This is the time to clear your soul
before we get just too old.
I will help you," she declares.
"Let us start today, downstairs."

He does not know what she fears,
as she looks on the edge of tears.
"It is not as bad as it appears."
He offers this doubtful assurance.
"I keep these things for insurance.
Do you know what a 2x4 would cost?
It would surely be money lost if,
carelessly, this leftover was tossed.
I know, dear, how you like things neat,
and how you would put things on the street.
Old but good things I cherish,
which curbside would only perish.
You have waited for me to come around,
especially the time I found
the wheel from an old barrow,

stuck away in a space so narrow
I would have had to crawl to get it.
Can you blame me when I said, 'Forget it'?

In truth, I have been working at this task,
perhaps not as quickly as you ask.
But we are of a different time.
In my sparse youth, even wasting time
was looked upon as a crime.
Imagine what scorn would bring
if we were to waste a thing?
An extra wheel for your wheel barrow?
It would take a mind mighty narrow
not to see the financial loss if,
in a week moment,
I chose to toss a gem
I may one day again use.

I know it is something to face,
this losing of the space.
I know it is a mortal race,
and I must pick up this laggard's pace.
When my head says, 'Throw it out,'
my heart keeps raising doubt.
Think of the brilliance.
This box of cardboard?
Do you think your soul can justly afford
to cut it up?
I didn't think so.

Ending

Gold, emergent from the western sky,
edged by cobalt and crimson,
lights the greens and yellow greens,
all burning along the maple's edge,
making the quiet, solemn song of days end.
And from deep within the shadows,
made even darker by contrast,
the sparrow
sends out the sound of endings.
All things moving in the wind rest
in the silent dusk.

Flowers Upon the Water

Her ashes cast upon the surface of the pond
gave rise to flowers,
all sitting in the light
in yellows and reds and violets,
in lilies and irises and lotus,
all birthed from her heart,
opening their petals to the rising sun,
and they were warmed,
and they remembered her,
and they flourished forevermore.

Festival

I remember you in the early days
at the festival of some favorite saint.
The streets were alive with dance
and music and children, pulling at their mothers' skirts.
It was spring, casting warm sun on young lovers,
leaning in to hold each other erect,
teasing with smiles and bodily twists and turns, a peacock's dance.
I remember foods cooking on open grills,
sending aromas, known to generations,
wafting through the air and over the heads of jubilant revelers.
Losing its sidewalk borders, the avenue had become the platform
for celebration.
Spring — and sausages in hand on a toasted roll — acted in unison
to warm the heart and to feed the soul.
Old men and women, with grins wide and deep, moved from one food cart
to the next,
masking the pains accumulated from walking these streets each day,
making their way to subways and buses, off to work, mostly laborious work.
But today is the day of the festival.

An old, tooth-missing, back-bent woman sold roses, one by one,
to boys sixteen to sixty, who make their presentations, a
mid self-conscious giggles,
to the eager hands of lovers.
I remember that clam or was it that oyster-shucking man, who, unaware,
or, perhaps, too aware of your charms, as he opened each bivalve,
handing over to your waiting fingers, the fresh, raw mollusk of your choice,
one after the other, well beyond what had been ordered.
I want to say six or twelve, but it has been too long ago to remember.

I shall never forget my astonishment as on this lovely spring day,
I watched you in your innocent engagement of the street vendor
in discussion,
as you helped him reduce his inventory.
The festival of Saint Someone continued into dusk,
followed by the warm, dark night,
when the large, overhead enclosures of the food carts began shutting
with a thunk of finality,
as vendors and helpers removed safety wedges from the front of wheels.
Thus began the removal of brightly-colored posters, adorned in crepe paper,
symbolizing the passion and holiness of the celebrated saint,
some to be saved for next year's celebration,
others to be pushed into large, plastic garbage bags,
pulled along the street from curb to curb by loyal parishioners,
elated at the success of their annual festival,
once again ushering in the start of spring,
a renewal of Hope, felt through their Faith, personified by the loyal saint
who had resided in the hearts of their parents and grandparents,
as far back as the old country,
and when the crossings to this new world began
to a country where believers could conduct festivals to saints
of their own choosing,
in their own way.
As darkness fell, the street emptied, and you and I, as did other celebrants,
went on our way, enriched.

Floater

She floats across the garden,
lighting first upon the most modest
plants, close to the ground.
Then, as if electrified,
speeds to the upper branches
of the Rose of Sharon.
Alone, no others join her flight.
It seems as if she is aware of me
as she sails across the space,
for the time, owning it.
She is the only occupant,
except for those hidden ants
and me,
and, of course, the bumble bees,
too busy to notice her or me.
Were I of a different faith,
she might be my mother
as she flies up over my head
and so close to the ground,
always looking back over her wing.
She is of a pleasant orange,
more modest
than the brilliant Monarch.
But it is her seeming awareness of herself,
living to the fullest
in this spring garden space,
that is remarkable,
a space she has made her own.

I move from the front stoop
to the gate upon which she lands,
before darting off again across the yard.
From behind the glass door,
I take one last look.
No rational man dare believe
that a modest, muted-orange butterfly
could have an awareness of living
and exploring and engaging
in flights that are at once
daring, humorous, and elegant,
and, more remarkable, having such stage presence.
Her performance lights up the entire garden.
Most rational men almost never
spend even one minute looking at a butterfly;
however, if they did see this butterfly,
they would believe that while hardly probable.
this particular butterfly might even have a soul.

Fan Club

I love having a fan.
It's cool.
I actually have more than one fan,
but I am not sure where the other ones are right now,
probably in the attic or cellar
or stuck away in some closet behind hanging dresses or slacks.
I do like fans.
They really help to stir things up, you know, clear the air.
I had considered starting a fan club a few years back but decided not to.
I just could not reconcile the various logistics problems
with a whole bunch of people jammed into my living room,
trying to have a meeting while everyone is showing off their favorite fans,
and how shiny and silvery they are,
and how smoothly each rotates to cool the whole room.
Plus, some of my friends don't drive,
and I had visions of them trying to lug a big, cumbersome fan
onto a bus or subway.
You know, they would not be content to bring a smaller fan,
especially to a regional, twice-a-year fan club meeting.
Face it: human nature.
Bigger is better; first impressions count.
Anyway, the idea just fizzled.
I must say that on occasion, I have regrets.
It might have been nice,
particularly for our spring meeting,
to have a special field trip type event
like a sightseeing cruise around Manhattan,
maybe on that beautiful sailing schooner
I have seen docked at the South Street Seaport.

Imagine how refreshing that might be,
a whole bunch of fans enjoying the brisk breeze wafting through their hair
while totally entranced by the sun setting over the Hudson River
with all the colors of the prism radiating through the air over Jersey City.
Anyway, it never happened.
But we grow and we learn. Some things work; some don't.
What I have learned most recently from the COVID pandemic, however,
is that some things are better rendered in a virtual format.
I have concluded that a virtual fan club is a much better idea.
Rather than a bunch of people jammed into one room,
blowing germs all over each other,
have a zoom meeting.
We all get to sit in a favorite spot in the comfort of our own home.

From Behind the Ice

"You may see me through ice cubes,"
sayeth the poet of mysteries.
"Expecting cobalt, I give you cerulean.
As to black, there is none,
nor do I offer white,
but gray — crinkled, crackled gray.
"Tell all," I prefer to say.
Once the sun was the sun,
now called the golden orb,
still taking its rightful run.
The poet,
no longer languishing
in mundane languaging,
hopes for a newer light,
exposing a brighter prism,
a more aesthetic sight,
perhaps a touch of symbolism,
a genuine poet's delight,
at least one spoon of cynicism,
then one spark to ignite
the birth of modernism.
You may see me through ice cubes,"
sayeth the poet of mysteries.
"Expecting illumination, I give you
words bent through troubled histories,
now of a different hue, one could say,
all shades of crinkled, crackled gray."

Good Night

My bed, my heating pad, and you.
No more be needed
in this good, nighttime stew,
all tucked beneath covers that warm,
protect arms and legs and hearts and souls
from harm.
January's sting is well above our heads,
beyond the roof, slanting to the north.
Winds whistle to prove their worth
from the west.
Making its way,
the snow holds for another day.
And when the sun is up,
and my creaking bones have had their rest,
there will be no rising without protest.
Yet in the dark, quiet hour
before heads are deep in pillows,
my bed, my heating pad, and you,
no more is needed in this good night stew.

Grandpa's Invitation

In time, we will come together again.
You will come to our house.
We will have corned beef and cabbage,
or shrimp scampi.
We will celebrate.
I will play and sing for you "O, Danny Boy,"
a plaintiff "Danny Boy,"
sung by an old man, whose tenor has left him,
but whose heart knows more, now than ever,
the hurt in every word.

Perhaps, we will sing together.
You will know in your heart those words we all will sing.
Adults will not be half drunk,
even though a touch might improve their voices.
We will hug to make up for all the hugs missed
by forces of nature and forces of our own neglect.
In time, we will come together again,
much wiser, having seen the alternative.
We have looked through only a keyhole,
a sliver of light along the edge of the door left ajar.

When all men and women must stand six feet from each other,
when playgrounds must empty,
when grandchildren must wave to Grandma and Grandpa
through the glass door,
there is anger and hurt and tears on the cheeks of the very young
and the very old.

All have reason to cry.
Those in charge lament with arrogance the limits of their control.
Armed with all forms of weaponry,
they stand in stupor against the wrath of Nature.

And yet, the generosity of Nature
also offers the brilliance that brings humility
to those who search for understanding,
that will return balance, the salve that heals wounds.
And every man,
who takes the time to watch his grandchildren on the seesaw,
understands life.

In time, we will come together again.
You will come to my house.
We will have steak or hamburgers or shrimp scampi.
I will play "O, Danny Boy" in a most plaintiff way
so that we may place in a forgotten closet
the sadness we have felt in our separation.

And on the upbeat notes we will sing our hearts out.

Grandeur Lost

There was nothing to match your grandeur in all your pristine beauty,
casting from your surface the most wonderful shapes of grey
of the bluish tone,
and of the melodies of violets and reds to start each day.
And how the sun played its golden colors off your surface
in the heart of the day,
turning its way through skies of cobalt, morphing into cerulean,
before sliding beneath your hill of purist virgin white form.
Now you lay along the driveway,
rimmed along your edges with the dusty charcoal of the final throws
of late winter air.
Yet even in your demise,
you will remain a memory as a beautiful, pure covering of the world.
For now, until we meet again,
we shall all await your arrival in new form
as you renegotiate your partnership with the sun
to once again make possible the rebirth of the garden.

Gray

When men can no longer say
which laws rule the day,

when the truth turns gray,

when there seems no relief
from loss of every belief,

when hope becomes grief,

when words once spoken in hallowed halls
are replaced by mindless catcalls,

when the code of decency falls,
and
the torch that once cast light
is used to stir up fright,
inspiring yet another fight,

when the belief in fool's gold
makes leaders' hearts go cold,
and treasonous minds grow bold,

those who distinguish right from wrong,
who believe still the words of the song:
"My country, 'tis of thee, sweet land of liberty,"
must vow to stand strong,
to tip back the scales and right
the wrong.

The tyrant's steps are easily traced,
yet,
it is in the moment they must be faced,
and
the actions of principled men embraced.

Heat

There was a time —
remember that time —
when summer sun tanned our skin,
just enough.
There was a time when April ended,
and joyful dancing began in the woods
and in the marshes
upon creeks that swelled with the incoming tide.
Anything that would float —
logs lashed together, large wooden boxes,
derelict, half-gone, bow-missing, winter-washed-up craft —
became our boat.

And May became our month of dreams.
The first was of that holy day at the end of June,
when freedom would be ours.
And all along, in increments,
the sun warmed our earth and our hearts.
On the barefoot run to the beach,
when an intense July and August sun
made black-top streets ooze tar
that would blacken the feet of those not nimble enough
to navigate up over the curb to step upon the cool grass,
then down onto the sections of streets, shaded by stately oaks,
then back up onto the next lawn and so on,
progressing from one cool lawn to the next,
running the three blocks from home until finally,
the first steps in the burning sand and then —
the rush headlong at full speed
into the cooling waters of Long Island Sound.

Ahh, Jubilation!

Aside from the possibility of burned soles from overheated road tar,
the sun and its summer heat were our friends.
We knew nothing of ozone layers, nor of melting glaciers.
It was a natural thing for nature to act natural,
as it always had since any of us could remember.
Winter was cold, and ice formed in the creeks
and on our windows and front doorsteps.
Snow, cursed by the grown-ups, was welcomed on school days,
lots of it, by the rest of us.

The turning of the leaves in fall, beautifully described by the poet,
was accompanied by the turning of our stomachs
at the thought of returning to school.
The heat of summer was associated with freedom to be outside,
to explore the "woods," to climb rock outcroppings,
that when seen looking up from the road,
promised a deep, hidden cave,
which had to contain at least one arrowhead,
left behind by the Quinnipiac,
to swim in the strong current at Mansfield Grove
that allowed one to float as if weightless,
and before entering the incoming breaking waves of Long Island Sound,
to grab hold of the fast-eroding sand banks which, thankfully,
still had enough substance that one could hold on to.

Fireflies came out at night.
We rushed with open jars that had holes poked in the lid for the captured.
Streetlights went on.

Jars with their few occupants were set aside.
Kick-the-Can was rescheduled for the next night.
Everyone went home to sleep.
We had no cause to dream of ozone layers
nor melting of the glaciers.

He blames. She blames.

He blames
She blames
Circumstances left untouched
He prosecutes
She prosecutes
Circumstances left untouched
He defends
She defends
Circumstances left untouched
Crimes are committed
Penalties are paid
Pain inflicted
Pain received
Forgiveness offered
Forgiveness accepted
Wheel turns slowly
Circumstances left untouched
He blames.
She blames
Circumstances left untouched

Acclimatization

So, what are you for?
As for me, I am not for
sunset at four forty-four,
which is about to occur,
Fall Back, a sad November event.
The word to all has been sent.
Pull up your pants; pile the wood.
You have put away all that you could.
The gray window each morning
serves enough to send the warning.
This is not fog, my friend.
This is frost,
with more coming around the bend.
Short-legged pajamas retreat to the shelf.
Drag out the wool to protect yourself.
All red and orange and played-out green
have gone to sleep, not to be seen again,
until next fall repeats the pain.
We will survive this long, dark sleep,
as we have springtime promises to keep.
But what of the here and now?
By this fire we make this vow.
Stop lamenting this loss.
Embrace the gain.
Your complaints are all in vain.

There is still the bright winter's sun,
even after first snows have begun,
white reflecting shadows of blue gray,
more poetic than the poet can say.
So, what are you for?
As for me, I am not for
ignoring realities that one cannot ignore.
What goes around, comes around.
All of the earth is common ground:
footprints on the grass, footprints in the snow,
truths that all men come to know.
The earth turns in its path.
The living will survive the aftermath.

Hide and Seek

If you can find you,
you can have you.
You are entitled.
Look behind the tree
or in the closet
or in the basement
or under a pile of old sheets or blankets or fallen leaves.
You could be a name written in someone's story
or in the long-ago records of the maternity ward of some hospital.
There may be mention of you in Saint Claire's old records,
stored in the basement of the church hall.
Any finding of yourself that might have taken place in school is over.
There are records,
but whatever parts of you that were found
are in your head, still.
Search old places where you might have found
and then left
a part of yourself.
You can search Google Earth on line.
You will see the paths you've traveled.
There will be new roads and buildings in the fields
where you twisted your ankle or fought with Billy
or met up with what's-his/her-name on summer nights.
You may not find all of yourself,
but there will be time to carry on the search,
tomorrow
or even tonight

before you fall asleep.
Don't forget the dreams.
They are always searching,
although you will not know what was found
until the next morning,
and even then, you won't understand, not really.
Most importantly, remember that Hide and Seek is a long game.
If you have taken a long time to hide things,
the search will be longer as well.
Never forget that whenever you find something,
do a little jig, and in that long-ago, sing-song voice chant,
"Found you, found you, ha, ha, ha!"

Holding Ground

There is no sadder sound than
Winter holding its ground.
When the time is right for the robin's song,
the wind still howls loud and long.
Trees cast shadows on still-hard earth.
Cold air forbids promised rebirth.
The sun, in waiting, hides its face.
The trusted crocus has lost its grace.
And water, water everywhere,
rolls down windows, off roofs,
and fills the air.
Bodies, hoping to cast off layers,
find no solace in April's prayers.

House Photos

On table tops, unused,
or on piano tops or shelves between things,
treasures, unnoticed,
faces, bodies from just a few years ago or old,
plain, having no meaning until a remembering heart
is stirred by the image grey or in colors.
In the time of my young, growing heart,
you fed me from your garden of rich, ripe tomatoes and wisdom.
Framed three inches high, you reach into my memory and soul.
We cannot be together
as once we were,
but you are in my heart.
I see you on table tops, unused,
or on the tops of pianos or on my dresser,
images, memories, real people
whom I had touched and held and kissed
and still hold in my heart.
I hold in my hand this silver frame
and within its edges, your image,
you and me together
in another time that will live in my heart forever.

How long do you think this lasts?

The final game of the season,
the ballet recital,
blue-robed first grade walks,
sand castles,
breaking waves,
and falling stars
and kites in northeasterly winds on Race Point
and holes in one
on miniature greens
and hikes on paths set aside for exploring
and the nests of almost-forgotten birds
and candles lit
for small breaths to blow out
and tears at strike-outs
and cheers at being among the champions
and processions of gowns of red
and then blue and gold
and trading two wheels for four
and short voyages for long
and more gowns of white
and tuxedoes for cardigans
and visits on the holidays.
How long do you think this lasts?

How Much Costs?

What price to pay
since deceit was selected?
There will come the day
after fraud was elected
that truth becomes gray,
rules of decency rejected,
giving despots their say,
and laws not protected.
When tyranny is the way,
for every lie the liar lies
before your very eyes,
what music shall we play,
a song to mourn
upon the soldier's horn
for all to hear, perhaps,
deep, sorrowful Taps?

Imagine at Eleven

Imagine that you are eleven, and you and your friends build
an underground hut
that measures seven feet long by three and a half wide
and nearly four feet deep.
Over weeks,
as the ground has softened by warmer temperatures and rain,
you dig day after day,
and then, when the digging is done,
you build the camouflage roof,
whose function is to provide the final closing in of a secretly solemn place.
It is in that space between the marsh and the "mountain,"
far enough off the path that no one would ever detect it,
especially with the careful job of the construction team,
who spread around those dry, brown leaves and twigs
so as to create the illusion of haphazard nature.

Imagine, carefully sliding that 2x3 sheet of plywood under the saplings,
ending on the edge of the dugout's easterly wall.
Imagine, when all the work was finally done,
and on a dark-skied April day,
with the rain falling and the wind howling,
you pulled back the plywood entryway,
pulled closed behind you,
leaving just a narrow crack that would let in light
and still keep out all but a few drops of rain,
hardly enough to be a bother.

And in this quiet, solemn place,
sitting on old blankets and cushions,
"borrowed" from home,
the feeling of complete aloneness,
away from the world in a space of your own creation,
you are free, plus, of course, anonymous,
because no one knows where you are,
and if someone who did not know you, discovered you,
then you could choose to tell them your name or not.

This is way beyond the hide and seek game that you used to play
when you were a kid,
when that feeling of great satisfaction in finding your own special place
that was secret
swept over you.
This was big time, home away from home stuff.
This was, in the most profound meaning of the word, Hut!
Neither wind nor rain nor chilly spring mornings,
nor, I would imagine, should an unlikely snow appear,
could the cozy security of this underground fortress be compromised.
Let the A bomb be dropped! Now there is a place to be safe.

In Soho: Flower Shops

On the corner at the edge of the sidewalk,
sit stands of roses and tulips and chrysanthemums and irises,
filled each morning
half emptied by nightfall.
The human heart,
given to its own ways,
will beat a path to flowers.
A corner flower stand,
open since the 1930's,
existing in the shadows
of corruption and wars
and meanness and street violence
that prove less permanent than the rose,
taken home to lift the spirits and to confirm
that the most elegant of nature's emissaries
lights up street corners and human hearts.

In the Early Days

In the early days,
even before the Revolution,
there was the gathering of the stones,
the stretching of the bones,
always for just cause,
on sleds fashioned by genius,
hewn of oak and ash,
waxed to glide upon paths of hardened ice and knee-deep snow,
tasks each boy would come to know.
Trees made tall and stout by time,
reshaped as humble homes,
seated on the edge of growing fields,
spread across the landscape,
a new world which promised survival for the prepared
and extinction for the presumptuous.
Walls with foundations deep beneath the frost line,
one side holding in the dreams of a brave, new frontier,
the other, holding out the despot's agents with muskets,
who threaten to breach the walls of free men
who have traded the fear of the monarchy
for the hope of a government conceived by the governed.
Stone walls do not a fortress make
but line the claim of the patriot's stand,
where he builds his home
and sons and daughters
and beliefs In the rightness of freedom
and the inherent dignity of all men,
a world where the only Monarchs allowed
fly across the fields of corn and
land on garden flowers.

In the Spring

In the Spring, we will go to the Met, you and I.
We will go down the West Side, and we will cut through the park,
emerging on the corner of Fifth Avenue.
We will cross over and circle the block and park in the garage
beneath the museum.
We will walk through that back entrance,
past the model of the Parthenon, displayed on a pedestal,
and we will walk through the halls of the Egyptians
and the Greeks and the Romans and the Romantics
and the impressionists and the early moderns, with their cubes
or wild beast colors,
and the later moderns, with their drippings and striping and dotting,
and those who say as close to nothing as possible in stainless steel,
and halls of armor, killing garb, seen aesthetically,
and tapestries, taken down from the walls and windows of monarchs
and holy men
and monsters,
and in the weaving, the heart,
finding its way through the shaping of the hands in stone and metal,
on wooden panels, on canvas,
conceived by minds connecting through the air surrounding artifacts,
shoulder to shoulder, epoch to epoch, all lined up in hallways and galleries,
illuminating the leavings of the minds and hearts and spirit
of the human race.

We will have a hotdog with sauerkraut on the steps of the Met.
We will do this in the New York sun, along with young lovers,
holding hands,

and young families with young culture seekers,
skipping the generous layout of stairs, cast in concrete,
to be climbed by the young and serve as seats for the old
in all but the most bitter cold of winter.
The same sun that shone on the souls
wedging stone blocks to form the pyramids
or down on craftsmen shaping the Cathedrals of Rouen or Paris
or Rome or Madrid,
shone on Monet's haystacks or Edward Hopper's cottages
or beaches on Cape Cod.
We will find our way back past the Egyptian display
and travel back along the West Side Drive as the sun sets over the Hudson.
I will remember Rembrandt's masterful eye,
painted in his self-portrait as an old man.
We will pass the exit to the Cloisters and once again, say,
"We should stop there again sometime."

Kite Flying

The day we flew the kite, Evan –
when you were just tall enough to reach up to the string,
and I was just limber enough to bend down to that same cord,
the wind swept across Race Point,
off the ocean,
across the sand dunes,
and over our heads.

Your small hands and my old hands fed out a bit of twine,
first, in small lengths, and then longer ones.
As the wind captured hold of those dreams of flight
that you held in your young mind
and those of mine in an older vessel,
dreaming together of a vision:
our diamond-shaped form with trailing tail,
sweeping across the sky,
moving from left to right and back again
in great swoops
of airborne poetry.

I was not wise enough
to guarantee at least one kite flying at Race Point
each summer, from that time on.
As in other matters of life,
traditions become sporadic,
somewhere between absolute and maybe.

Small hands grow larger,
and if the dreamer of dreams is touched with good fortune,
so, too, are his visions of the possible.

The dreamer of dreams can have the curiosity of Icarus,
but must include within the equation,
the melting point of wax.

No human quality can carry more weight than that of courage.
When wind from the ocean sweeps across the sand dunes,
the well-prepared kite,
held at the correct angle to the wind,
will take flight.

The ill-prepared kite will rise a few feet above the earth,
making ever wider circles,
until it crashes headlong into the sand.
It will do this over and over again.
No amount of courage will cause the ill-prepared kite to fly.

The wise kite flyer will prepare well his instrument of flight
and will study with care the direction and velocity of the wind.
The wise kite flyer will determine which elements of the journey
he controls and those to which he must learn to adapt.
The wise sailor uses the strength of the wind against itself
by tacking and achieving an even greater speed forward.
The wise judo master uses the weight and thrust of his opponent
to tumble him to the floor.

The young navigator of the landscape
will make of adversity an ally
and will grow, not in spite of it,
but in response to it.

Courage is best achieved in the presence of fear,
unless you are very different from all who have walked
this path before.
You will grow, stumble, get up again,
face moments of doubt, have successes and failures,
and be presented with great opportunities.
When that happens,
although you may not know
from which direction the wind will present itself,
you will have control over your own preparation
to ride the currents.
Embrace your considerable talent.
Be more thankful than boastful.
Respect your art, and learn your craft,
so that when the wind blows your way,
you will be prepared to ride the currents
in great swoops of airborne poetry.
Know that you are loved and will always be more
than the sum of your failures and successes.

Love,
Grandpa

Keeping Things

How could I throw away shards of green-edged glass
that sparkle in the light?
How could I not see far off stars that give brilliance to the night
on walks along quiet country roads?
How could I not see the distant sky and clouds
reflected in the puddle left from yesterday's rain?
What has been saved of the great old maple stands as sentinel,
despite the cutting pain,
now gone branches, yielding shade to passersby,
nesting places for the sparrow and the dove,
a meeting place for those in love.
Despite its loss, this tree does not die
leaving that to the passerby.
There is still the challenge each day,
what to save, what to throw away?
Most things that leave or stay
will do so without my say.
Yet when there is a choice,
how could I throw away
shards of green-edged glass
that sparkle in the light
or fail to see stars
that make elegance of the night.

Libra

Libra sees the sun and rain,
the hot and cold,
the yes and no,
the good and bad,
the happy and sad,
the strong and weak,
the fast and slow,
the come and go,
the now and then,
the modest and vain,
the pleasure and pain,
the one and many,
the honest and corrupt,
the kind and mean,
the living and dead,
the fire and ice,
symmetry and asymmetry.
Libra searches for the fulcrum,
wake midday,
asleep midnight,
weighing every wrong and every right,
when in the dark,
seeking light,
while in the light,
seeking the silence of the night.
"Ah, the ambiguity
of it all," sighs Mr. October
as he sits on the toilet
and blows his brains out.
"Wait a minute!" cries his inner voice.

Libretto

Attention!
Were you or one of your loved ones on or near camp Lejeune
between 1953 and 1987?
Shingles doesn't care.
Only pay for what you need!
Shingles doesn't care.
Your price only $9.99 a month.
Your price never changes.
Young people, having a good time with insurance!
Young people!
Good time!
Insurance!
When you have nausea, heartburn, indigestion, upset stomach, diarrhea,
people who know, know BDO.
Do not take this medicine if you are allergic to it.
Side effects can include heart palpitations, elevated blood pressure,
and, in rare cases, death.
Shingles doesn't care.

Love at Thirteen

I carve your initials in this tree,
taking a stance for all to see,
and within the heart, I add my own,
chiseled away, each cut well known
before the start.

In my dream, you stumble upon this sacred oak
and cry out, moved, "I did not know!"
Silence is as silence does.
Beyond the cutting, no words are spent.

Walls of stone and walls of space,
walls of turning away,
walls of prisons, self-imposed,
walls shielding broken hearts,
walls built by assumptions untested,
walls that never part.

I carve your initials in this tree.
It is a song to you from me.
There will be aging of all three.

You and I will grow up.
Our tree will expand its girth.
Letters will blur, exposing in time,
their true worth.

How long for chiseled hearts to heal?
How long for human hearts to no longer feel?
How long before silent loves mend?
I ask not for myself,
but for my best friend.

How Slowly Turns the Night I

How worrisome my plight.
How yearned for is thy sight.

Marsh at the Turn

Muck, black as tar,
nourishing marsh grass,
edging restless creeks.
Seagulls circle and dive.
Fiddler crabs scramble.
The quick survive.
The slow gamble
to catch a bit of sun,
an ecosystem thriving.

Spring has begun.
Still waters driving
ice flows nearly done.
Warm waters begin their run,
passing islands of solid earth
home to the staunch tree,
boulders of weight and girth,
buds waiting to rise.

The land warms by degree,
slowly, beneath bluer skies,
a place to feel and see
through young impatient eyes.
Fast footsteps on the bank
left by invading youth,
send fiddlers to their holes,
as surely did the gulls.

No time to ride the ice,
once guided by sapling sculls.
Winter has passed.
Trips down stream require
different hulls.
Rafts will spring from
youthful skulls,
logs gathered, bound, and tied,
pine boards scavenged and nailed,
as elegant a craft as ever sailed,
buoyant enough to float,
a test for boy and dog.

With added weight, a sudden drop,
decks awash, a sinking in the bog.
the crew abandons with a hop,
maiden voyage a dismal flop.

Mid the silent setting of the sun,
Pilgrims follow,
the winding path home.
Gulls turn their fishing to the sea.
Fiddlers emerge for the day's last run.

Melody

As darkness lifts,
robin, blackbird, and thrush,
in chorus and alone,
put silence to rest,
and from the puffed-out chest,
melodies sweet
greet the rising sun,
and smoke floats up from chimneys,
and the sparrow and finch and soprano and bass,
as needed, join in,
and the sound of the barking dog and the whirring motor
and the non-sound of the deer,
stepping out from behind the pine grove,
all flowing like a stream
amid sun rays and moisture, still clinging to grass.
And high above, sound, muffled by distance,
makes itself seen in the contrail streaming from behind a silver vessel,
a bullet with wings, holding on its surfaces
the reds and golds of the sunrise and in the shadows,
the cool blues of the sky and clouds, now white, now violet.
And flights among the branches
and flights among the clouds,
all in melody and silence,
all in time and space,
the day begins.

The Maple

What winds have beat against its weathered bark?
What sun has worked between its rustling leaves?
Elements as witnesses to history's arc,
and the cloak each generation weaves
along sideroads that once were mud
or deep in fields once cleared for planting.
Corn and beets and brave patriots' blood
stood tall against the despot's ranting.

Memories of the Wind

Cat paws upon flat silver blue
in patterns, curvilinear and true,
to the winds seeking design's most gracious way,
leaving modest waves lapping quietly
against the quay.

And flags, taking turns,
hanging limp and lifting, shifting,
leading edge against the breeze,
and beneath all, the placid sea
and above, the cloudless sky
and below, swans swim by
and above, gulls that fly
and geese, dressed in black,
formed in a V,
some heading out,
some heading back,
each riding in the contrail of the other
as would any loving brother.

All of this the eye has seen
on a day in early spring,
when along the edge of the bay,
all in harmony, chose to sing.

Memory: Your Gift of Chimes to Me

Beneath the chimes, a melancholy song,
turning in September's prophetic wind,
shadows of the setting sun
cast long shapes of trees already thinned.

Perhaps you will direct the wind
to move the chimes in a loving melody.
As each chime casts its spin,
searching for sorrow's remedy,

your presence felt in wishful hope
keeps you with me for this time,
far beyond any reason's scope.
My heart wishes for your rightful shine
among the stars.

Would that I had a dream to relive,
I would take away your pain.
I would ask that you could forgive,
and I could once again
erase your tears with a chocolate bar,
had you not traveled away so far.

Mind Chatter 2

What does it matter,
this mind chatter?
How many times
do we confess our crimes?
And imagine, for every sin,
God is sticking in a pin.

Why should he bother
if he has Father Reilly in the box
with his scary talks?

In truth, we need no judge,
since we remember every smudge
the eraser leaves behind.
To thy own self be kind.
We have been designed,
as has all mankind,

to be just and forgiving
Of ALL the living.

As for the dead,
who have nothing left to dread,
keep them forever in your heart
and, for a time, in your head.

Night Shoppers

Waiting, silent,
save for muffled rumbles on the distant road,
passing dark figures,
traversing asphalt on a mission.
Dark against dark against darker,
burdened on the return,
passing beneath the lights,
night shoppers,
clinging to bags of bread and eggs and cheese,
head back to the nest
to care for the young.
The witness waits in silence
for his passenger to return.

Morning

Morning is for the meadow lark,
whose song penetrates the dark,

and all those lovers of the rising
reds and golds and mesmerizing

mists that float over the hill
and settle in valleys to fill

thirsty ponds and creeks,
to sooth half-awake cheeks

of those who make things grow
in gardens they have come to know,

as did those who came before,
whose soul at its very core
was of the land.

The growers stand apart,
practicing their noble art

with trusting heart and weathered hand,
and the mind, hoping to understand

rhythms that make the earth turn.
Hopeful men, yearning to learn
secrets.

Here is one, known by the modest fox,
who would pass nature's test:
take what is needed, leave the rest.

Greedy men, more snake than fox,
have set their short-sighted clocks

to harvest riches for today.
Take all. Put none away.

How will tomorrow's youth fare
when searching for clean air
and
water to serve the hardened soil
on which the growers toil.

Blue morning sky's light,
in which the fisherman takes delight,

his once bulging, bountiful net,
now surveyed with deep regret,

as the catch dwindles year by year,
and
new generations come to fear

the death of a way of life,
that cuts like a rusted knife.

The sea may empty in its rise
amid citizens of all nations' cries.

The sun, which rose to warm the earth,
now burns to answer
man's self-inflicted curse.

New England Spring

In time, the sun will win against the dark clouds.
The warmth will replace the cold.
There will come a time again when
I will sit in the chair on the front lawn,
the one that swivels,
and I will look northeasterly
through the sky hole in the trees that line
the outer edge of our yard.

I will see birds seeking a place to nest for the night.
I will see the silver streak of airliners
heading north to Canada,
or northeast on a path that will take them up the East Coast,
out over Cape Cod or Maine or Nova Scotia,
over the North Atlantic to Paris or London or Madrid or Rome or Venice,
sweet Venice.

I will plant my feet on this lawn,
just turning green after the winter's brown and white freeze.
And swiveling left, I will take from the table my drink and my journal,
in that order.

The great human experience of hope born of the Renaissance,
the rebirth of the land and the soul of man is the subject at hand
and so, the Spring of all things blossoming
and expanding
and brightening
and coming back to color,
lives unto itself and would proceed,
absent the witness.

Yet, I in my swivel chair,
noting the turning green of the grass and the trees,
the blossoming of the crocus,
the coming to life of the rhododendron,
and all things visible and invisible,
sit and take notes,
as if this were the first time
I had ever seen a NewEngland Spring.

Observations From a
New England Yard

A low treble hum, interrupted bass,
silver, stretched out oblong,
moving in and out of clouds so light
as to be invisible against the cobalt sky.
Stainless, its longitudinal lit by the western sun,
its latitudinals serving as wings, fall into shadow.
And as if called upon from stage left,
the drama of souls, lifted above all of the earth,
and, most particularly, all of New England,
whisper off, northeast,
looking down at the Connecticut River,
looking up at the pamphlet, Paris by Night,
looking down at Cape Cod, Nova Scotia,
the ultramarine North Sea with churning white caps,
looking up the canals of Venice.
Shades snap closed on the starboard side
as the sun in its western setting beams its full power,
its last burning of the day.
"And on the port side, ladies and gentlemen . . ."
The still awake
note the drama of reds and oranges and violets bleeding into one another,
with holes remaining for the blue,
seeping through deepening purple on its way to black.
Glasses tinkle; food trays slam up and down;
seats make the reclining sound,
a snapping in place,
the final sounds for now, amid the dimming of the lights.

And tree frogs sound out so as not to be forgotten, and fireflies circle,
disappear and reappear feet away
as if they could share the stage with Houdini,
and song birds send back and forth the plans for the night's lodging.
The reply seems in agreement,
but none outside of the communique can be sure.
Still, beauty is in the melody that carries the message,
and as if in a ballet,
the arc from tree to tree in swoops cutting through the air
now quiet as the settling of the wind takes place.
And far above the clouds, souls sleep,
dreaming in anticipation of adventure
as the sun rises with the landing.

Of a Winter Afternoon

Writing words with the light at my back,
hoping at the start that December's bite
is held harmless by the glass,
glazed by knowing hands,
four panes in a row,
four rows tall.
No warmth more consoling
than the sun on my back
when writing on a winter's afternoon,
looking out on sunlit lawn and cloudless skies,
needing but the landing of the sparrow
on the black branch
for poetry to find its way.

Of all the grey that can invade the day,
when rain turns ice
and trees restless in the wind,
shadows dark and deep
and longer with the day's history,
taking its rightful stance,
for this is its time, after all,
yet in the freezing left behind,
all diamonds sparkling
in the morning sun,
enough for poetry to find its way.

When the land has turned white,
and the moon owns the night,
and all sounds are muffled between
the earth and stars,
there is wisdom in sleeping
for the bear and the rose,
and souls looking out through glass,
four panes in a row,
four rows tall,
enough for poetry to find its way.

Passing Through

There is a time of day
when the road is grey,
when sunbeams are few,
and the sky abandons blue.

All contrasts disappear
as dusk draws near.
Night follows close behind
as the heart hopes to find

its way down the darkened path,
ablaze in righteous wrath,
lamenting what has been lost,
Fate's sorrowful cost.

For in the turning of one day,
young prayers, "Let her stay,"
echoed through the universe,
fearing the dreadful curse.

Every form of "Please" was tried
when mercy chose to hide.
Young lives pay the toll
that shakes their very soul

There is a time of day
when loved ones slip away,
and the road does not turn back
as night turns grey to blue to black.

Picture This

Picture this, if you will,
when all the world is still,
just before the birds begin to sing
to herald the rising of the sun,
and grass and leaves and all uncovered things
have upon them the dew found in the leaving of the night,
and souls moving about,
neither looking nor thinking
of the magic in the east,
are lifted, nonetheless, into the day.
You take your picture: of a place, of a moment, of a memory,
frozen in the lens.
It is of a life frozen in recognition,
like the deer, frozen in his tracks upon confronting the hunter.
Now,
you are the hunter,
seeking not the deer,
but elegance, ecstasy,
the moment, aha,
when all falls into harmony,
reasonable enough to move the heart,
which stands by in the prescience of the only relevant sounds,
the song of the robin,
the beating of the heart
and the click of the shutter.

Potter

How will you shape this clay?
As the wheel turns toward you and away,
what will your fingers say
about the center
that wobbles on this day?
That truth is in the shape of nothing,
the shape within the walls,
the shape that makes
of spiritual mud
what the artist's heart recalls,
sustenance for body and soul
held warmly within the walls,
soups and stews and chowders,
recipes from your mother's day,
from head and heart to hands,
the shaping of a vessel,
deep and wide in palaces and humble huts and all between.
What shall be held in this empty space surrounded by gracious walls,
round as the earth is round,
made whole in the fire,
held in hands of the young and the old
and of citizens of the world, shaped by history?
How will you shape this clay
as the wheel turns toward you and away?

Pull Up the Ladder

"Pull up the ladder,"
sayeth the short-sighted.
Our country is full.
Extinguish the flame.
Darken the harbor
through whence we all came,
huddled deep in the hull,
or in staterooms on deck,
each soul making claim,
hearts escaping the wreck
of despots' hold
on the fragile neck,
of starvation's toll on every name,
of those who travel
in countless forms of fear and shame.

Our country is full.
Extinguish the flame.
Darken the harbor.
We are not to blame
for every country's madness,
for every refugee's sadness.

Remember, we got here by ourselves,
and perched here upon our rightful shelves.
Lay down the torch; lift the ladders.
Corrupt leadership defines what matters.
When compassion calls, build more walls.
Our country is full; the light shatters.

Poverty Hollow Waters

How black the stream in Aspetuck Gorge.
Modest bubbles head south,
resting in the deep, dark mystery of still pools
among boulders of containment.
The heart is treated to the crashing and melodic mist of the falls,
fed by Winter waters that flow on in their Winter depths,
heading toward Spring, when they will
serve the trout, the fisherman, and the water bug
as swollen creeks, lined with the diamond sparkle of the sun
on ice-framing creek banks and the tops of boulders.
Away from the light,
in spaces between hillsides and shadowed pines,
frigid water slows,
wearing down the boulders of a million years
and the ice of last night's freeze.

Still, it is the blackness of the surface that eyes, in vain,
attempt to decipher the remnants of dark things below:
old, curled leaves and sticks and stones and winter colonies of life,
floating around or burrowed beneath the mud for protection
from the torrent.
There is the elegance of dark ribbons, twisting and turning,
moving and settling behind curves
to leave mounds of ice, clinging to the winter grasses,
and then flowing on through the landscape edging private yards,
passing under bridges, and then growing more narrow
and winding its way into the deep woods,
eventually to settle into a pond or sink deeply into the earth
or to find its way to a place where swans will swim on its surface
and deer will come to its edge to drink,

and fish of every type will swim beneath the surface
and both on the flight south and the glorious return in the Spring,
entire flocks will find refreshment,
sustenance begun before the dawn of man.

Pragmatist's Soliloquy

(Ode to the Bard)

Tomorrow, Tomorrow, and Tomorrow is Wednesday
because today is Sunday.
Yesterday, Yesterday, and Yesterday was Thursday because — that's right–
today is Sunday.
Today is the day that God rested after he created the universe.

In the larger universe, it is more difficult to know when Tomorrow is
because time is all caught up with space ever since a fellow named Albert
Einstein came along.
Before that, say, in the seventeenth century, one could,
with some confidence, say,
"Tomorrow, Tomorrow, and Tomorrow."

Now it is not so easy.
Also, consider, right here on earth, when they are waking up in Paris,
because it is Tomorrow, people in New York will not see Tomorrow
for five more hours,
so, it would be more accurate to say, for example, right here in Paris,
"Tomorrow, Tomorrow, and Tomorrow will take place
over the next three days,"
but if you start saying that in Paris and then fly to New York,
Tomorrow, Tomorrow, and Tomorrow could take longer.
If you sail on a ship, it could take close to a week.

If you are expecting something to happen after Tomorrow, Tomorrow,
and Tomorrow,
under such conditions, it will probably happen at a creepy, petty pace.

If you are young, or if you are old, you will just have to get used to it
because this system is going to go on until the end of time,
or at least until nobody keeps records anymore.

I know all of this may sound very esoteric.
The most important thing to remember is that a lot of foolish people
don't know how to use their time and live lives of quiet desperation.
To hear them tell it, you would realize that their stories are a lot of
rhetorical jabbering,
often loud and too often furious.
Frankly, no one need listen to these idiots because it means nothing.
At least, so far it means nothing.

It is like a poor player who struts and frets his hour on the green
and can't sink a simple putt.
I think we have already established that it means nothing.
I have tried to tell this tale, not like an idiot,
but with as little drama as possible.

The reader, as all writers should know,
has just a certain amount of time to allocate for reading.
Most importantly, the reader prefers completing his reading in one day.

Stories that go on until Tomorrow are inconvenient,
and those that go on Tomorrow, Tomorrow, and Tomorrow
are just dreadful.

Purple Says to Yellow

Stand by me, and I shall set you free,
yet, if we try to blend,
that will be the end
of you and me,
and in our place, a brandnew grey,
that we may sway either way,
chosen by what we hope to say,
and yellow says to purple,
"If I am the sun in children's landscapes,
the light found in near round shapes,
what sadness would be for all
if purple rain was to fall,
not just upon the likes of me,
but over every field and tree,
filling streams to overflowing,
ending every flower growing
in every garden on the earth,
challenging every birth
and darkening the sky
and the hearts of evil men
who with their evil pen
send their youth to war.
Of what consequence is
purple over yellow when it falls as rain?
Of what consequence is darkness over light?
Of what consequence is purple rain
as it falls upon the children of Ukraine?"

Premonition

How fatally the despot misjudged
the quiet rage in
fearful hearts
that he inspired
throughout this divided land.
Now stands the premonition,
older than before the Crucifixion,
when evil men end innocence.
In time, innocent men end evil.
Corruption can be talked away
for some time, but not all time.

How fatally the despot did misjudge
the shortness of the rope,
guiding him to redemption,
all smiles and surety,
as if this day would never end.
Fools once fooled
shall be forever fooled, or so it seemed.

How fatally the despot did misjudge
the fickle ways of the fooled,
as one by one, they will utter damning words
as in the turning-away deeds of Judas,
and all accolades,
once spoken in the feeding of the bully
will be withheld by now silent mouths,
speaking in shadows,
nodding heads.

"We knew it all along," they will say.
"He was a fake; we knew it all along.
I tried to tell my friend.
I just knew. Somehow, I knew."

Real Deceptions

A vision appears true,
spread out in cobalt blue.
I drive on River Road,
alongside flowing waters,
and through the trees, a placid scene,
surrounded by camouflage green,
sunlight reflecting
what proved to be a spoof,
what appeared as river was, in fact, a roof
appearing so blue
I envisioned it as true,
flowing only in my mind,
directed by my misled eye.

Off beyond the forest high,
above the tree line,
wings of a hawk
in a frozen glide,
catch zephyrs upon which to ride
seemingly forever.
This sudden second,
when I spied upon the window pane,
a speck of darkened dust,
spread in happenstance
by a mysterious hand,
inspiring once again,
in a fooled mind,
a vision most grand,
of a modest kind,
dirt in the shape of a hawk
upon a window pane.

How you shall swoop and dive into and out of gentle winds,
you, solitary leaf.
You should have fallen to the ground.
You catch my eye as you fly.
I cannot determine what depravity
allows you to defy gravity
as you do.
Still, after a joyful time,
watching your dance,
I come to wonder what circumstance made this magic,
and then a line, all silver in the sun, made your secret undone,
a remnant from a spider web,
tethered to the deck chair,
floating in the wind, invisible to my eye,
still holding you aloft to perform the ballet of the sky,
curled up remnant of a maple leaf,
dancing to wonderment and deceit.

Refugees All

Refugees all,
big and small,
short and tall,
Sean and Saul.

Melting pot
burns a lot
when stirred with
Intolerance.
Despots cannot hide
their desire to divide
with words preaching
hatred.

Remembrance 2

I remember pushing you on the swing
that hung on ropes from the aging, pink dogwood
that grew in the front yard.
I would push you back and forth,
sitting in my lawn chair,
just within reach of the plastic seat
that surrounded you and your protruding legs,
and I would twist the four ropes
until they curled around each other like a loaded spring,
and I would let you go with a powerful push and a half twist
to set in motion the swinging, twisting, roller coaster ride through space,
and you would yell out in unbridled joy and occasional terror.
After some spins, I would remember the caution.
"You know, I read that spinning a young child excessively
could injure the brain,"
Grandma cautions,
and so, for a while, it was just back and forth,
as high as the chosen branch would allow,
and then, after a while, I would ask, "How are you feeling?"
And when your eyes looked ok and your dizziness went away,
I gave another twisting, swinging push,
and you squealed,
and I sat in my lawn chair and reached out,
giving a push when you had coasted to a near stop.
On most days,
it seemed that the coasting and the spring air and my aging bones
and your adjustment to the ever-quieting swings
inspired the occasional blinking and then closing of the eyes.
As for me,
it was enough that I could be with you
in those days.

Reunion

We are old now.
If I were to see you
and you me
on sidewalks we once
shared,
you would not know me,
nor would I know you.

Yet, should we meet,
each of us knowing
that the other is in the room,
we would find each other.
I would find you in your voice,
and you would find me in my voice.

Waistlines and bent shoulders
will serve as camouflage,
yet,
some twist of our heads or angle of our smiles
would remove the first blankets blocking recognition.
covered by the graying of hair not yet lost,
or the ballooning of the belly,
the wrinkling of the skin,
the slowing of the walk.

But if I am ever to know you again,
it will be by the unique light in your eyes,
however dimmed.
They will not have lost their link to your soul,
nor to your identity.
What greater hope can the seasoned searcher wish for
than to find and be found
by an old friend.

Revelation

If you like the shape you're in,
keep drinking that tonic and gin.
If you wish your belly would shrink,
perhaps it's time to think.
If you can stomach moderation,
you can avoid the humiliation
that comes from a body so rotund,
it could speed the way to moribund.
A fat brain is worth the weight,
if used to guide your fate
in a manner well-reasoned
by one who has been seasoned,
not by rosemary, salt, and thyme,
but by passages through time,
lessons learned through error,
corrections to avoid the terror
of the saddest sin
of paying no attention
to the shape you're in.

Road Side Farm

It is in the land
and
in the blood.
It is in old names
on old signs
on old country roads.
It is in old, black,
disintegrating
photo albums
of older generations.
It is old initials
carved into
ancient maple trees.
It is the old, overgrown,
hard-packed road
that rims the field
of waiting corn
and beets
and cabbages.
Left aside,
confirming the history of this road,
are old, rusted tractors,
transformed into bronze-like,
patina-covered sculptures.
This old road maintains its history
of heaving and sinking,
as years of spring flooding
and winter freezes
leave their marks,
as do the hoofprints of cows,

obscured in the rich, black mud
in pens of chewed pine boards,
bound by chicken wire,
and everywhere,
in gates and between posts,
the omnipresent X,
serving as brace and design element,
conceived even before
the father's father.
Grey and silver, shiny cars
pull up to the market.
Bins of freshly-picked vegetables
of reds and yellows
and myriad shades of green –
not behind plastic wrappings,
nor under fluorescent lights,
but in a simple shed
under the shade
of that old maple tree,
which has witnessed
generation after generation,
coming to squeeze and tap and shake
what has been gathered
for the family meal
And kids pour from the back seat
to get a better look at the cows,
with their insistent snouts,
pushing stubborn calves
away from the hole in the fence.

The perfect summer squash
and string beans and apples
have been found.
Reluctantly, all pile back into the car
and drive off,
having entered the history
of the place,
having gathered enough for a
remembrance
like all those who came before,
those who worked the land
and those who came after the harvest.

Rhythm of the Marsh

Land and sea meet at edges of soft sands
that follow tides along the ever-changing floor.
Land and sea meet at hard edges of imposing walls of stone,
where waves explode into mist
and settle back into the following surf
and then back further into the endless ultramarine of the sea,
edges, soft and hard, tranquil and fierce.
but of the marsh, there is another plan,
where the tides of the sea
and flowing, slowing rivers seek openings in the land
and forming creeks commingle with the land,
flowing in snakelike ribbons of water,
reflecting their silver at high tide
and retreating back into shallow waters,
edged by rich, black, umber banks of mud,
where fiddler crabs sun themselves
and watch for the daily raid of sea gulls or herons or crows.
And between creeks and tributaries,
in the brilliant yellow-green of spring,
standing tall and flowing in harmony with the wind,
marsh grasses form camouflage for the multitude of critters
whose history has followed the ebb and flow of this rich sanctuary
since before the time of the mad men with bulldozers
and artists with brushes or poets with pens,
and for the time that is now and is still to come.
The destiny of mankind is the same as the destiny of the earth,
which shall be foretold in the destiny of the marsh.

Rise in the Road

There's a rise in the road that wasn't there before.
It is clear to me now at eighty-four.
Once favoring fast, now I favor slow.
With still so many steps to go,
a road that chooses to incline
chooses as well its own decline.
The walker while at the crest,
arms and legs and mind at rest,
looks at the way still to go,
perhaps 200 yards or so.
Measuring by eye is but a guess,
but I have done that more or less.
All the days of my life,
amid harmony and strife,
in time, this walk will end.
I will seek the lawn chair,
my springtime friend,
and observe, with profound interest,
this day's weary end.

Shakespeare in Eighth Grade

"Tomorrow, and tomorrow, and tomorrow creeps in this petty pace
from day to day
["Oh, my God, Sally. I am so bored. Send me a note."]
to the last syllable of recorded time.
["I am dying here, Sally. Do something. Fall over.
Pretend an epilepsy fit again."]
And all our yesterdays have lighted fools the way
["Her skirt is so short. Has she no shame?"]
to dusty death.
["Nice move, the coughing fit and the rolling back of the eyes. Perfect.
Who are you sitting with at lunch?"]
Out, out, brief candle.
Life is but a walking shadow, a poor player that struts and frets his hour
upon the stage,
["Martin looks so-o-o amazing today."]
and then is heard no more.
It is a tale told by an idiot,
full of sound and fury.
["Do you know what she is talking about? No? I mean really?
Her shoes are so yesterday"]
["I am so bored. What a waste."]
signifying nothing."

Shrimp Cocktail

Shrimp cocktail, a screwdriver,
standing at the window of the beach club,
looking out beyond the rocky shore,
standing tall.

Shrimp cocktail, screwdriver,
grey sports coat,
looking out,
prideful smile at having arrived,
finally.

Shrimp cocktail, screwdriver,
back bent by years of feeling less
among all others,
one inch after another.

Bent shoulders, grey sports coat,
the modest swagger at the bar,
the look out at the horizon
through the finest floor-to-ceiling windows
from where the successful stand
at tables holding dishes of shrimp cocktails,
sipping screwdrivers.

Standing erect at being called "Sir,"
still not sure the bartender means him,
still not sure.

Silent Tears

Beneath covers,
undetected,
wet pillows,
hearts too hurt
to share,
are muffled cries,
a loss too great to put to words.
The world above the blankets
is too cold.
Things that happen there hurt too much.
Little heart, beyond your awareness,
big hearts sob for your brokenness.
Resilience is what they say of young children deep in despair.
"They will get through this," they say.
You will, without choice,
in time, cry at sudden moments,
hidden from the other, quiet, sad ones,
embraced by the loving hearts
that surround you like a winter overcoat.
You will feel alone.
Still, every heart in every man and woman,
if told of you,
will weep for you.
Among all the sad happenings,
they will weep for you,
and I will cry for you,
and in my failure to change your loss,
will hurt in my heart for evermore.

Perspective

The red-breasted robin upon the lawn
might seem majestic to you,
but to my brother worm and I,
we prefer the robin in the sky.
To you, the robin makes of the spring a time to sing.
My brother worm and I prefer
the robin with the broken wing.
And when the robin is off on a certain day,
blackbird will come by to dance and play,
sometimes singing in the dead of night,
causing for every sleeping worm, a terrible fright.
Life looks very different
from below the ground,
especially when one of us is found.
We have yet to devise a plan
to protect us from the brutal fisherman,
who rejoices when he gets us whole,
the better to hang from his fishing pole.
And then, of course, the toads and moles,
breathing down our holes
with their slimy tongues and smelly breath.
Consider the reason for our sad frown.
Every clown looking down
can send us off to an early death.
As to questions of a full or empty cup,
for all creatures, life is harder looking up.

Solo

The old man sings.

In silence, aided by the dark, the back row departs.

Hesitantly at first, footstep follows footstep
in a drum-beat cadence, one behind the other, down the aisle.

Emboldened by those behind, the next row, in order, exits left,
rounding the last seat, stepping lightly.

The old man sings, arms outstretched, heart on fire.

From random seats,
muffled coughs break the darkened silence
between the notes.

The rustling of stiff evening dresses,
partnered to navy blue jackets,
whisper,
avoiding recognition as they slip away.

The space cools as the warmth of bodies
leaves only the echo of the single voice
that bounces off empty walls.

The old man sings, his arms outstretched, his heart on fire,
his eyes cast upward above the blinding stage lights,
and into the darkness.

Sip and Drip Art History

So, tell me, Vincent, dear,
having given up your ear,
what else is there to fear?
Whisper so
no one will hear.
Pain, neither plain nor clear,
describes the lonesome life
mid solitude and strife.
You could not make yellow
yellow enough,
and
despite your deep sky view,
you could not make blue more blue.
How could you know in your deep despair
that the world would someday care.
Works you could not give away,
now copied in reverence and play,
all paints supplied and canvas, too,
just searching for another you.

With all good wishes,
Sip and Paint just misses.
Getting drunk and removing your ear hurts,
despite how it may appear,
what genius they feign,
without, of course, the pain.
All thirty "Starry Nights" pretending,
feeling only spirits ascending,
same size, same colors, same broken strokes,
and radiating stars.

How far their compass has gone astray,
missing what you tried to say.
To be you is to be unique.

All lined up to sip and play
is a tragedy in its own way.
Sober or wobbling drunk,
try with all their might,
they cannot make of themselves
the creator of the Starry Night.
It has been done in Provence
and again, in fifth grade and again, in a dull education class
and again, in the Senior Center and again and again and again.
A bad copy is never cool.
Better to get drunk and
fall off your stool,
or better still,
take up pool.

"Wait!" sayeth the critic.
"Is it not true
that every artist, save a few,
has learned from those who came before?
Who knows what will open
a creative door?
History notes that part of the deal
is for great artists to steal.

Song of Wonder

Let us write a song,
you the melody, I the words.
We will find sound and substance in the wind
and in the rhythm of waves
and in the click clack of heels
upon the sidewalks of New York City and Hong Kong
and in the rhapsody of horns on Parisian streets.
Let us write a song that hears the silence before and after darkness,
the sound of young men marching,
and the squeak of tank turrets turning
and the giggles of lovers in the Tuileries or Central Park on spring blankets
and the soaring of buzzards over blood-soaked fields of mud,
the modest chirp of summer evening song birds
and the crunch of autumn leaves
under the feet of old men walking country roads,
the wail of the new born,
the shuffling of feet, the clapping of hands,
the swishing of blue robes cast into laundry bins,
the muffled sounds of beating hearts of the old and the very old
and the brand new,
and outside this encapsulated space,
the sounds of the sirens of the world.
We will write the words and melody of endings, befuddled, inept, sad,
still missing what the mind really means.
We will explore the notes and chords
that emulate the explosions of hope
that reside in the hearts of the left-behind.

I will use my words to speak of the earthly dreams of souls,
leaving behind what was thought to be lost in its entirety.
Yet, it will have to be your melody
that moves every man's passion toward solace
and the uplift of the human spirit.
Your sound must be like those that echo off the walls
of the greatest gothic cathedral,
to be as the faithful imagine is found in the harmony of the chorus of angels.
Let us write a song, knowing of all that we have missed.
Let this be only our first song,
a song of wonder.

Sparrow's Belief

It is said that the sparrow is
a loving bird.
You may watch him if you doubt.
You will see him step back
from the feeder
when the cardinal or blue jay
muscles in.
The sparrow will remain himself,
watching, waiting, assessing.
When bullying and gluttony
have had their way,
the sparrow will perch himself on the feeding ring
and without ruffled feathers or flaring wings
will quietly feed.
He has no illusions of claiming first bites
nor of inheriting the earth.
He simple surveys his size and appetite for a challenge
and determines an uprising would be folly.
His kind have outlasted all with enduring patience,
gathering together as kindred spirits,
enjoying the wonderful directive:
"Love each other and multiply."
His dominance in numbers on all of the earth
confirms for him that what he has heard,
perched on the branch beside the open window
of the Holy Promises Church that
"in God's kingdom, even the little birds will be taken care of."

"Little bird. That's me," he said. "That's me.
Blue jays and cardinals are not little birds.
While these bullies fight each other,
I will be hidden in the rich, deep coverage of the pine tree,
making love with Susie.
We will be back.
I promised to take her out for dinner afterwards."

Speak Quietly of Death

Speak quietly of Death,
for if you say its name aloud,
it will hear you.
Do not act fearfully
over Death,
for it will know
that you have noticed
what was to be kept silent
until it was,
of its own accord,
announced.
Use other words:
"To pass,"
"Passed on,"
as in a train passing through the station
on its way elsewhere,
and all along the platform,
non-passengers wave
to the one looking out
from behind the window.
In your thoughts,
substitute words of Life
for words of Death.
Be kind to the silent movement
of words within your mind,
directing all that is in your heart.
Allow life to take up the greater space.
Hold hands in the light
and through dusk into the night,
knowing that what you have written
cannot be erased.

Spring

When morning forgoes its bitter sting
and robin announces the coming of spring,
the sun, now beating long and strong,
sets in time for the tree frog's song.

All that have been sleeping, now awake,
each in its own time for nature's sake,
creatures in dark places, once abiding
in the new days light, come out of hiding.

Waters, stopped by winter's cold,
now run free, swift and bold.
Black ooze that lines the marsh's creek
becomes the home fiddler crabs seek.

Mankind, venturing from its own dark cave,
still learning what to spend and what to save,
celebrates the turning of the earth,
and, if wise, protects eternal rebirth.

Yet,

among the creatures, it is man
most likely to create a plan
that fouls the creeks and greys the air
and in his haste, forgets to care.

Starting Over

When the edge cannot be found
between the stupid and profound,
Start Over.
When, after you have made your case,
the next best step is to erase,
Start Over.
When you have called for hope,
but meant a call for help,
Start Over.
When you think your mind is still alert,
yet know that to think is to hurt,
Start Over.
When the words that once flowed from your pen
only happen now and then,
Start Over.
When all the words you used to rhyme
have lived out their time,
Start Over.
When all the dreams that could not be,
wished beneath the wishing tree,
have gone to sleep,
join them.
You are eighty-three.

Stay Put

Stay in your room, not mine.
You are contaminated.
Stay in your house, not mine.
You are contaminated.
Stay in your yard, not mine.
You are contaminated.
Stay in your neighborhood, not mine.
You are contaminated.
Stay in your town, not mine.
You are contaminated.
Stay in your state, not mine.
You are contaminated.
Stay in your country, not mine.
You are contaminated.
Stay on your continent, not mine.
You are contaminated.
Stay on your earth, not mine.
You are contaminated.
Stay in your universe, not mine.
You are contaminated.
Stay where you belong.

Stay with Me

Do not turn away before I leave.
Be with me with all your heart.
There will be time enough to grieve
when, finally, we will be apart.

When we are together, yet alone,
you next to me and I to you,
trust in the seeds that have been sown.
Trust in our love, strong and true.

Do not escape into that space
neither here nor there, between.
Be with me in all of your grace.
Let us by each other be seen
for what we are:
two hearts and souls in flight,
still in the sun, fearing not the night.

Still Growing

You know you haven't long to go
when your patience shrinks, and your ears still grow.

Nothing can make it clearer
than a broadside look at yourself in the mirror.

Ears, not the only feature that grows,
one could also make a case for the nose.

What you wish would grow, namely, your hair,
can't be found anywhere.

In truth, it has only left your head and
migrated to your nose and ears instead,

long, curly squiggles in black and grey,
to be trimmed every other day

and then forgotten. Instead,
let's consider what's in our head.

Never mind

Summer Night

The silence of a summer night,
when all that once had been in flight
rest hidden in motionless trees,
at peace in summer's gentle breeze,
all tucked in until the morning.
When sun and mist first meet,
inspiring the dove's early rising,
then goldfinch and sparrow,
whose first flight, straight and narrow,
join the new dawn melody,
celebrating the revelry,
flitting tree to tree on rested wings,
searching what the new day brings
beneath the ground or peeling bark,
worms and grubs pulled from the dark,
all creatures with a beating heart
will recognize this daily start,
this rhythm of nesting in the night
and waking with the light.

Sun Descending

What will you do before the sun descends?

Will you move to the rhythm?

Or if you are reluctant

to dance with your feet,

will you dance with your heart?

You may not think of being cheerful in the snow as being hopeful,

but it is.

Even as the sun descends,

your faith promises

that it will be back tomorrow,

and you can build your snowman,

who, without moving,

will communicate joy

through black coal eyes

and a red carrot nose

and wiggly stick arms.

What will you do before the sun descends?

Live every moment of your precious life.

That is the recommendation.

Tending the Fence

There are truths a fence man cannot abide,
imperfections a fence man cannot hide.
Among repairs that can wait,
I would include the crooked gate,
for despite its leeward frown,
'tis very common in this town.
Still, above all, what matters most,
is to have a level post.
When what a man might hear
is corruption to his ear,
consider as well, what can make a fence man cry
is an assault on the eye.
When a post planted long ago
abandons what is true
and in its right or leftward lean
has abandoned what the truth might mean,
consider how the old fence man with old fence senses,
having spent a lifetime mending fences,
will for the longest time stand,
level in hand,
seeking to understand
all that must accrue
for a fence to go askew
and knowing, as well, if he should wait
he might also lose
a still-working gate.

The Best Route

How often we have traveled this route, wondering if it was the fastest.

There was a time when distance mattered.

Which way required more miles?

But time has taken over as the arbiter of efficiency.

In our more thorough days, we imagine segment against segment.

"Ok, from home to the corner of Sport Hill is eight minutes.

That is like from home to the corner of Judd and Stepney."

"No, I think a little shorter — maybe, seven or even six."

"Ok, but then from the four-way stop sign to the Parkway

is ten minutes flat.

I have done it in nine."

"Ok, but from Judd and Stepney, up Hiram Hill to 25 can be 8 to 10."

"That seems a lot, but look at how much further east I get on the highway."

"Ok, but by the time you are stuck at the light on 25,

I am already past the light on Jefferson

and on the highway at 65 miles per hour —

four minutes from the Jefferson entrance to the 25 entrance! Ha!"

"Oh, yeah, in seven minutes, I was down to the Merritt

and a lot farther east than you would have been!"

"And then from the exit down Nichols to the grandchildren's house —

well, that would be the same for both routes —

but what if we took the back way down 25

and cut across to Second Hill Road over to Nichols and then to Main.

I'll bet about 14 minutes from 25."

"We should try that some time. We could probably save 2 minutes."

"Maybe. Depends on the traffic. Certainly worth a try."

"Sport Hill is so pretty in the fall."

"Yeah, so is 25."

"Sure, but you're going so fast, you hardly see it."

The Fountain

On the day when the memorial fountain
that was to flow forever dried up,
dry leaves fell onto dusty cement,
twisting and turning in the breeze,
providing no relief from the sweltering heat.
Caretakers on the day shift
as well as on the night shift,
had failed to replenish the reservoir
that provided cooling waters,
pumped through hoses to the bubbler
that rises, fills the basin,
and sends waters cascading down the stone face
to be recycled over and over,
losing some to the sun,
yet gaining from the rain or the hose of the gardener,
until now,
when the rains have lost their once-recognizable logic,
and the guardians of replenishment have slept through their shifts,
and all that once drank from the fountain
to cool their bodies
or to heal their troubled hearts,
turn away in sadness and loss.

The Other Shoe

Waiting,
for the other shoe
to drop,
too much time spent,
waiting,
for the other
shoe
to
drop.
Too many thoughts
of the dark,
long
shadows,
cast beyond the edge of reason.
Too many dark words
chasing
dark thoughts.
Too many circles
rolling out paths,
repeating
dark words inside,
over
and
over
and
over.
Too many pages
pock-marked staccato:
sadness
sadness
sadness.
What's next, undefined,
waiting for the other
shoe.

The Pennant Is Dropped

The pennant is dropped.
The mooring left behind,
captain and crew, hoping to find
a friendly sea, a gentle wind,
a balm for the troubled mind.

Songs of a long-awaited spring
replace winter's melancholy sting.
Paths followed by the pilgrim's feet,
or trimming of the sheet
start with the freeing of the cleat
and the clearing of the mind.

The wake so clearly leaves behind
turbulence of every kind,
sends ripples out along the way,
forming waves that caress the distant quay.

Of all the words that a man can write,
or all the words that a man can say,
none will be wholly right.
Of all who venture out on any day,
or mid the darkness of the night,
climbing waves or hills of grass,
on foot or with a pen,
know before you start,
a wise compass is the heart.

The Swan

A solo swan drifts upon the currents of loss
and floats in and out of places of sweet remembrance,
where two reflected side by side in shadows of the pines,
where there were no dreams of one without the other,
nor winter winds to dodge,
nor spring rains to tolerate,
before the sprouting of flowers along the bank of the lake,
nor floating along a shore beneath falling autumn leaves,
nor aloneness looking at the summer moon and stars,
when there was belief in together forever.
Now the solo swan has his reflection in the lake
and visceral memories of his soulmate,
and in the dark of night a dream of being with her still
for evermore.

The Wave

There was, years ago,
as I was speeding by,
an old man, bent,
trudging this old, country road –
a Pole
or an Irishman
or a German
or a Jew
or a Russian –
a foreigner, for sure,
'twas easy to say,
by his particularly foreign sway,
and the crook of his cane
was of a foreign twist,
and there, upon his non-cane wrist,
a sparkling amulet,
perhaps prayer beads
or medals
from a far-off war,
the one that took Jim
away
and made of Walt
a drunk.
I would answer the old man's wave,
thinking it queer
that a stranger
would greet a stranger,
but that was years ago.

The old man is gone.
I have ended my speeding,
traded for more reflective ways to take the road.
More weathered and wise,
from beneath the hood of my winter coat,
a nod,
and from the non-cane arm,
a modest lift
in the coming and going of a wave.

The Visitation

Riding air currents above the tree tops,
slicing through grey-white clouds,
the hawk lands upon the branch of that old, dying ash,
then perches upon the wire attaching our home
to the rest of the electrical world.
He sits on a branch from which he can
observe us having dinner on the deck.
I know he is watching us with his flawless vision.
He spreads remarkable wings
and floats off through the woods,
gracefully weaving between the trees,
now beginning to bud in their early spring-yellow greens.
We marvel.

The Wind

The wind appears as the sailor's friend until it kicks and blows.
The wind appears as a soothing voice until its dark side shows.
With cobalt skies behind, a cumulus cloud bank grows,
not, it seems, of the gentle kind described by gentle prose,
but of the type the sailor knows that sends a tragic charge below.
Ships leaving unsuspecting hearts behind
to bask in the gentle breeze of a summer's eve,
neither dumb nor blind,
yet believing that the wind will never change, that all winds are kind.
The wind appears as the sailor's friend until it kicks and blows,
While the naive pretend that a peaceful wind forever flows.
This is how the air must move, from east to west or west to east.
Destiny still hopes to prove
that
when threatening winds have ceased,
enlightened hearts are soothed
as hope and compass guide the sailor home.

The Work

How long is the journey
to learn to write
words that none can understand?
Four years of poetry school for some,
endless years of living for most,
calloused finger tips from searching
reams of obfuscation,
laid to rest,
over centuries
in typefaces named for empires
and other idiosyncratic choices,
by scholars in every land,
in every time.
As I write, I see the bright orange sun
setting behind the scraggly trees of winter,
falling, finally, behind the now-compressed
dark forms along the horizon.
How can I find the words to describe this event,
as if something greater than a common sunset is happening?

Trees

In their quiet presence,
rooted in history,
witness to the growing and the turning,
instrument to the music
blowing through empty branches
like strings of the harp
or the reed of the clarinet,
strokes of black against cobalt,
leaning toward white,
from thick, heavy strokes,
the chalk on its side
tapering to one dimension,
smaller, smaller, and then again and again
until lines are so light,
they dance in the gentlest of breezes.
The first to turn free
their golden leaves for flight,
the first to turn to diamonds
in the first freeze of winter,
the first to welcome the return of new life,
all green to fill the space,
to cast the broader shadow,
to host the home of the sparrow,
still.

Unbound

Unbound by knowledge,
urging caution,
inspired by hopefulness,
he prepares the feathers of flight,
the heart that will guide the journey,
leaving the grave earth
to enter the sky of brilliant light,
bathed in shades of cobalt,
traveling through mists of grey white
presented as markings along the way.
If south is his home,
then north must be his destiny.
All elements of and surrounding the earth shall stand as witnesses,
and the wind will assist in the rising,
and the Pilgrim will make peace with all elements that would advance or
end hope.
The heart rises above modest hills and mountains,
through and above clouds,
to settle, at last,
in the presence of pure light,
in the moment of pure joy.
Hidden in the joyful celebration is the flower, about to fade,
as truth will force its way upon dreams of the young.
The ways of the world will not change to suit your visions.
The melting point of wax cannot be changed,
despite the enthusiasm of your heart
nor the careful planning of your voyage.

Your greatest wish,
as the truth of gravity fulfills its promise on your free-falling body,
is that your soul will remain whole and prophetic.
and, if not you, then some future pilgrim,
inspired by your belief, courage, and hope,
will rise through and above the clouds
to float as closely as one dares
to the golden light of the sun.

Turning a New Leaf

As to turning a new leaf,
to reduce future grief
and for the greater good,
more water, less food.
Reduction seems to be the key
to achieve a lesser me.
I must establish in my head
the limitations of daily bread.
How well I have come to know
all types of the modest potato:
baked and mashed, "frenchly" fried.
How often has my stomach lied.
A few more will do no harm.
Oh, how gluttony does charm
the ever-aging, growing boy,
working so hard to destroy
a waistline of modest reason,
appropriate for every season.
Now, I would be a fool
to be seen bobbing in any pool,
yet not for looks this mandate holds,
nor just to erase those extra folds.
The working of the heart will ease,
as will the load upon the knees.
'Tis true that I may never water ski,
being more than eighty-three.
Still, I may lose the fat man's frown
in the mirror when looking down.

This message may seem trite,
as if conceived on a sleepless night,
as if by one who fell out of bed
and landed hard upon his head.
Please, that thought you must erase,
as this is not the case.
The explanation can be found
in the desire to be less round,
and, hopefully, there is this added perk:
my heart will have to do less work.
Should I not take heed, I will be a fool
(I know I should have used "jerk",
but just wanted to see if you were paying attention).
So, in summary, let me say
this shall be a new day.
Enlightenment is not just for the mind.
To the body as well be kind.
But let there be no notion
that I will give up flammkuchen.

Upon Rising

And when the darkness gives up its hold,
when shades lift in quiet tones,
and light presents itself,
first, in modest risings over horizons behind dark, flat, mountain forms,
on ribbons of light, flowing into the growing blaze that is the lake,
when all that is touched by the light rises,
the sound of new life from open windows of maternity wards
and
sounds of children dying in homes made into battlefields,
sounds of pine branches moving with the wind,
the crash of waves off rock ledges along coastlines,
the tenor warming up,
the Father screaming
the Mother screaming,
the children crying
what will the sun find upon its rising:
the whispers of men conniving, pulling shades to block the light,
anxious for the coming of night,
the roars of rejoice around the diamonds of ten-year-olds
swinging bats,
the click of a door lock,
muffled sobs from beneath the desks?

Pop, pop, pop
is how they tell it with bulging eyes and shivering souls:
the whimper of grown men forgotten behind bars,
the whimper of children under blankets,
a cacophony of beeps and screeches and motors humming
and errant sounds all rising
from between steel and glass and concrete cities,
rising as elegant, refined stalagmites of human invention,
some standing as mirrors,
reflecting the sky and the white clouds and the yellow heat of the sun,

and on the lake, the sound of oar locks in a rattle of wood against metal
and the swoosh of the tips, moving through water
and the deeper, slower, heavier tone of a simple boat moving forward,
he in the rowing seat, facing backward,
she in the rear, facing forward in youthful admiration
on its way to committed love.
And the thud of shovels hitting dry, hard dirt
in what had been verdant land
where tomatoes and corn had once grown,
and the whoosh of waters, flooding through broken levees
and around sand bags,
and families yelling from atop their roofs,
small voices drowned out by the cic, cic, cic of a helicopter
or an outboard motor.
Beneath the thruway, the cardboard shelters and trash can fireplaces,
and above, the voom, voom of cars,
carrying employed accountants, salesmen, teachers, carpenters, lawyers,
and all forms of those connected to the commerce of the world,
and below, the near-silent sound of rolling up sleeping bags,
children playing dodge ball in the play yard,
screeches and screams and laughter,
the tap, tap, tap of the blind man's cane crossing Fifth Avenue.

In silence, a jetliner rolls down the tarmac, slows, then roars up,
then silence again, aloft, the whoosh of wind in a circle,
lifting homes and all things not secured to the earth,
whales breaching off Cape Cod and all capes of the world
in Grandpa's ocean, suddenly rising,
youthful bathers riding breaking waves upon beach sand,
extending out in its sun-bleached ochre,
darkened by the wetness of the sea,
with each retreating step, the sound of feigned, joyful terror.
Turntables creak and squeak

and turn thumping, hissing diesel engines facing Chicago
to facing California. Great ships scrape up against concrete piers,
the gesture of swinging arms directing, then silent palms held up.
Engines throttle to a stop in the profound contrast of quietude.
Footsteps shuffle and clank down aluminum gang planks.
A whistle, weakened by the air and space between there and here,
sounds its declaration.
Fields fill over time, all white flakes falling in silence
to cover the pockmarks of the earth,
from silence to whipping wind,
also, in white with a stinging bite.

What will the sun find upon its rising:
the cadence of young men in lockstep battalions,
backs erect, chins forward,
death's assistants held diagonally hand to shoulder,
moving forward in syncopation with the waiting for the chosen enemy?
Prideful trumpets and drums, French horns and flutes
paint across the sky the colors of the flag,
embraced decades ago and stored in lockers, on flagpoles,
and in the hearts of those marching and those watching
and those made real only in memory.

A well-oiled track is silent as its velvet curtain gathers at either edge.
Stage lights give rise to human discourse,
changing pitch in murmurs and shouts,
in tears and laughter,
in the solitude of the soliloquy,
in the majesty of the chorus.
What truth is found upon the stage
that echoes mankind's love and rage
made word upon an honest page?
Voices aimed at golden altars and tabernacles,

awaiting deep sonorous replies,
a bass, surrounded by the treble harmonies of angels,
voices reflected off walls,
escaping through open, stained glass windows
into the air occupied by the beeping of taxi cab horns,
the kerthunk of a great tree,
falling in a forest somewhere on the earth,
the desecration of the top layers of the world,
laid bare in search of the glitter of diamonds, the warmth of gold,
the rich, black ooze of oil and copper and all elements,
surfacing amid the sounds of celebration,
and on either pole of the earth, the sound of drills,
whirring to test the age of ice as the splash of one ledge sends ripples
through the ocean and around the world, and crackle,
the sound of trees on mountain sides ablaze
sends shivers to those paying attention.

Gardener, tend your garden.
Protect your knees at eighty.
Your heart is cared for in your passion.
Tulips grow at the turn of your hand.
Upon the setting reflected in your tired eyes,
the sun fades into the night.

What will the sun find upon its rising:
the Yavapai, the people of the sun proud in times before casinos,
my country, tis of thee, hiding under desks in grade three,
dreamers of a more just world bending knee on gridirons.
And before the sun, the fisherman sets out for a fair casting
the nets of capture and survival that float beneath the surface of the sea.

What will the sun find upon its rising:
the flow of rivers and all that ride the current,

commerce in pursuit of profit,
paddle wheels in pursuit of the lifting of the heart
through finger picking jazz upon a river boat,
mud slides, lava flows, abominations of the once trusted earth,
and such profound sadness
as grand and modest castles are buried,
fields of wild flowers, host to wild horses and foxes and ant hills
and grasses, moving with the wind that whispers
as if the song of the symphony has been turned down,
Purple Mountains' Majesty, found in real stone,
sitting upon the horizon, mile after mile, at dusk and dawn,
appearing like cutouts against the luminous sky.

In chambers of mahogany and polished brass,
voices make claim on the rational
while madmen seek to resolve the trauma of their early years
while extending the trauma of history,
written in the blood of all souls,
in the languages of all and any selected,
without exception to race or nationality or gender,
requiring only the ability to die by the sword or assault rifle or tanks
or bombs.

What will the sun find upon its rising —
a picnic in the Tuileries along the Seine or in Central Park
along Fifth Avenue.
The sky is blue; the sun is golden;
children run after dogs that run after frisbees,
gliding through the air by big brother, mother and father,
heads upon pillows reading and dozing off, one eye open.
water preserved in plastic,
destined for eternity,
rolling upon the verdant grass and in the waves of the seas,

gathering in a place offshore,
where currents collide and resolve their drift,
and lettering, elegant and promising,
refreshment in French and German and English and Spanish
all swirl
in keeping with the nature of the movements of the plastic tide,
young, black man, broken taillight,
crying, "Mama" in the street,
dying from a knee to the throat,
saving siren too late.
the clip-clop of hooves upon stones,
pulling the black hearse of our captain,
death by bullet to beliefs,
clip-clop, soundless wheels beneath golden carriages,
moving the offspring of parasites who carry crown and gene forward,
amid the grateful cheers of the poor, amnesic historians.

All retreat to the beach to the scream of "Shark!"
on a sunny day in Chatham.
All stand in the gallery of the mahogany house,
the scream of "Shark!" muffled by the sound of wind and waves.
The click of the finest leather shoes echo against
highly-polished, hard, oak-wood floors,
then go silent in the plush carpet of violet.
From the righteous statesmen there is silence
while the world awaits inspired eloquence.
There is silence before lunch.
There is silence after lunch.
There is the sound of a collective sigh, waiting.

What will the sun find upon its rising:
the whir of drilling through the deep ice of the winter lake,
the plop of the lure and sinker as it descends through frigid waters,

and men in sheds, heating the space with human breath,
warm gloves, insulated parkas, and the passion of tradition,
handed down through generations,
and tilapia and perch and their cousins and forebears,
even before the Pharaoh greeted the early rays of the sun,
reflecting off the surface of the Nile.
What memories of nets are stored in their schools,
whose silent parade twists and turns through friendly and unfriendly
currents, generation after generation — the clank of welded wire mesh
closed to hold salted herring or blue fish or pogeys
and cast into the sea by hopeful hands,
to be hauled up on another day off craggy coasts of North America
and Australia and the United Kingdom,
sharing the seas each day with earth doctors in white,
taking the temperature of the warming waters.
And across open, reserved plains, thundering hooves
of what is left of burnt umber waves of bison on the run
or standing at frigid attention in the snow.

What will the sun find upon its rising:
the cacophony and symphony of the earth,
in its timeless turning amid miracles and madness.

Waiting

In the shadows,
the deep, dark, dank, day-after-day shadows
in the lee of the house and on the north side of the ancient maple,
spread out in its obstinance, the snow, the snow that will not go.
And all accumulations left from the plowing,
holding forth,
accumulated on the edges of parking lots,
darkened at the edges by the cinders of passing cars and dirty air,
piled like mountains, stubborn, proud, even in its slow melting away.
The snow that will not go,
diminished in the struggling edge between late winter and early spring,
using the still-freezing nights to reconstitute itself.
And as the grey mist of morning lifts,
patches, whitish black, emerge
to signal not yet, not yet.

Wind Dancer

Who could not love
this delicate, purple
wind dancer.
Thin membranes
allow the light,
once yellow,
now trading cobalt for violet
and
turning back again in the breeze,
zephyrs so quiet,
only the hummingbird
hears stems moving against
rich, bright green grass,
bending west, then back to east,
casting shadows,
confirming the light.
How tall you have become so early
while Spring is still unfolding.
The Rhodies are nearly full.
Your kindred chorus,
who share your markings,
add their spindly elegance,
filling in the waiting space
to your left and to your right.
The story goes that you carry within you
the wisdom of the flowers
as you come early and stay
long enough to inspire
the building of the garden
to its eventual splendor.

Winter Fire

There is consolation in a winter fire
the night before the snow.
Small flickers lick the logs,
promising flames as the fire goes.

And you tucked in upon the couch,
and I in a close-by chair,
tending logs, stubborn at the start,
as I shift each with patient care.

Beyond the window, night air
has brought the bitter cold,
yet this fire lacks a certain flare.
Flickering flames will just not hold.

A good fire requires good design,
with logs set at proper angles,
and a good starter would be fine,
all squished in a neat diagonal.

Paper that reports political crimes
would render flames of a liberal kind.
For this we choose the *New York Times*
for the best fire one could find.

When Tree Frogs Go Silent

When tree frogs go silent
and fireflies go dark,
hardly noticed,
the slipping away,
when the wind from the south
becomes the wind from the north,
and the skin, once cooled
is chilled and stung,
the leaves have converted
as promised.

Morning frost sparkles
on windows and plants,
and the bones of old men
creak from the bed.
Well-worn slippers head south,
following the compass
that ritual provides,
resting by a window,
inviting the sun,
blocking the wind.

And on the walk, it is to be
on the leeward side of the trees,
toward the warmth, away from the breeze.

In time, the day will warm,
the frost, having sent its warning,
will melt and change its form.

Just before dusk,
chipmunks will scamper,
no time to waste in the gathering.

Winter will be upon us in no time,"
says the Almanac
and the old man's bones.

"But that is a long way off,"
says the dreamer,
who revels in the turning
of green toward yellow and red
and their offspring, orange.

It is Autumn,
glorious Autumn,
and those who prefer fall
as in fall is not a rising,
it is a fall.

There is more wisdom in the squirrel
and birds of every kind,
who, rather than weep for losses,
as the cycle turns,
prepare without regret
for the next season,
and the wise man takes stock
of his wood pile
and his blessings.

Winter Lingering

What greyness do I feel
in winter's mighty grip,
when the sun sets
and starts to slip

beyond the darkened hills
as part of my soul sinks.
The maples stand in silhouette
against cerulean yellows and pinks.

Cold black settles in stages.
Breezes, tolerated in the sun,
nip and bite at toes and ears,
all human comfort undone.

What winter steals, it offers back –
nights of solitude, diamonds in the sky.
If wise, we join the rhythm of the earth,
allowing our souls to comply –

thickening of the blood, slowing of the heart,
gathering of hopes, gathering of needs
before the snow transforms,
before the blossoming of the seeds.

Winter

When winter is a season of the heart,
and the sun has chosen to depart,
and the cold upon the cheek does sting,
all hope rests upon an early spring.
When winter is a season of the mind,
and joyful thoughts declined,
replaced by those which brood
by ignoring every gratitude.

When snow has been laid upon the ground,
and acclimation of the soul is found,
and blood, once running thin, has thickened,
as the now resolute step has quickened,
light seen amid dark trees
casts upon the ponds deep freeze,
all diamonds and sparkles of all shapes,
giving brightness to sleeping landscapes.

When winter is a season of the earth,
there is no end to birth.
Buds rest beneath the frozen ground to wait,
as in the past, their fate,
and all else rests in the plan.
All creatures, grasshoppers to man,
through living will learn
that, gracefully and in balance,
the earth will turn.

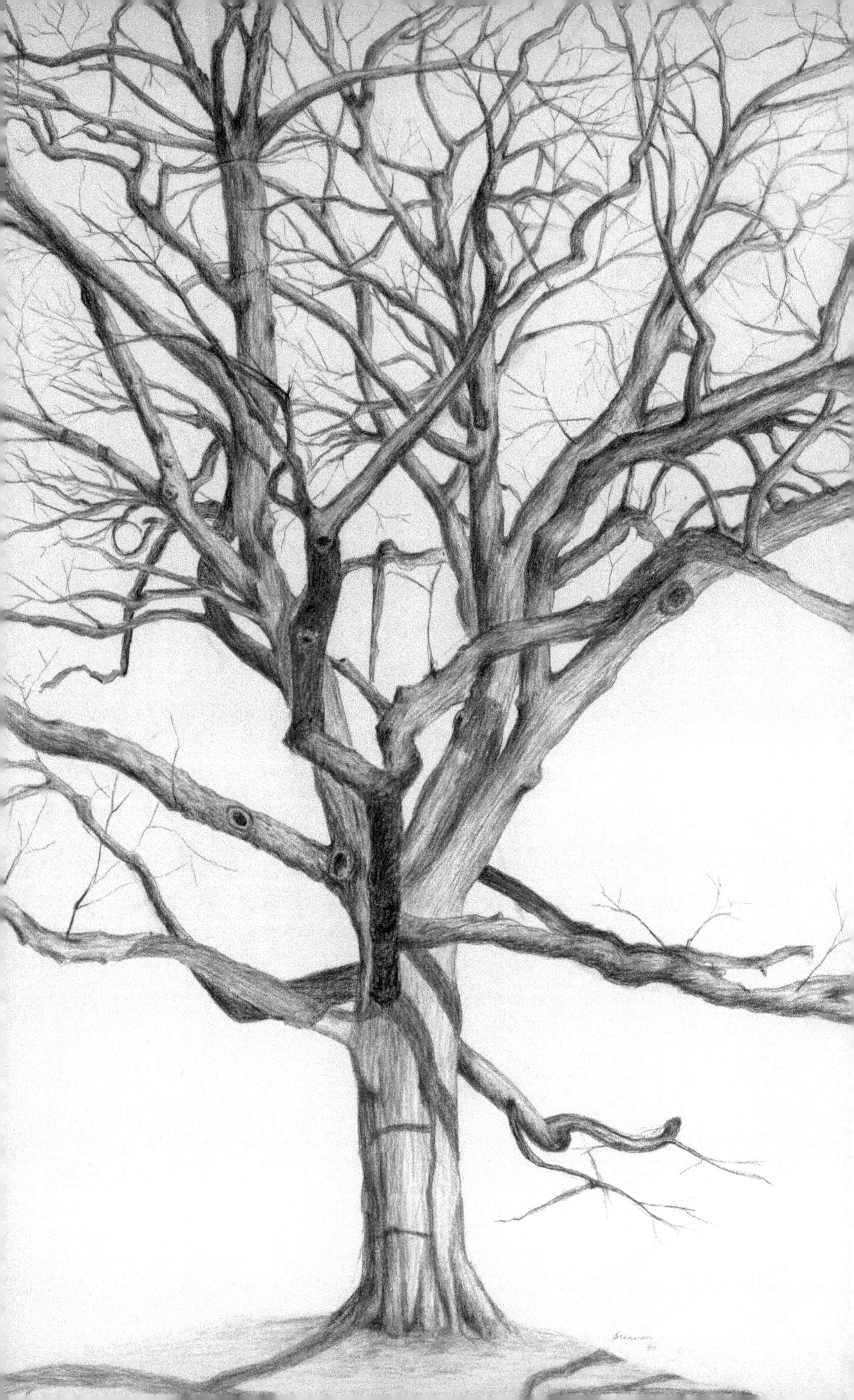

About the Poet

WHILE CONTINUING HIS WORK as a painter and constructivist, Robert Brennan shares his observations of the world through the language of poetry. Beginning with simple word sketches from his deck in rural Connecticut and sail-aways along coastal New England, he has turned his eye in many directions, from the sights and sounds of the landscape and the sea, to observations of the inner life of souls trying to navigate a world full of wonder, mystery, tragedy, and joy. His words make note of a world he sees and imagines, often in the rich imagery that binds his love of the visual and the written form. Brennan found that with words, he could expand his range of personal expression, at times in combination with his artwork.

For more than twenty years, Brennan, a prolific, award-winning freelance painter, served as a professor of art at the University of Bridgeport and art department chair for ten years. He also taught drawing at the Silvermine School of Art, New Canaan, CT and served as the K-12 art coordinator for the Darien School System.

He received his BS at Southern Connecticut State University and his MA at Columbia University, where he also pursued doctoral level studies at Columbia Teachers College, majoring in Painting and Printmaking.

Brennan maintains his studio in Easton, Connecticut, where he lives with his wife Patricia. Brennan's artwork can be viewed on his website, therestlesseye.com. Google him at artist Robert Brennan. To preview an exhibition of his abstract paintings and constructions, search on youtube Abstract Art Variations by Robert Brennan.

Acknowledgments

A SPECIAL APPRECIATION to my wife, Pat, for her great generosity of time and effort and caring, for her great skill as an editor who remained true to every word, while never missing the correct place for a comma or a semi colon, who, with great sensitivity, advised me in the creation of unique configurations in the layout of the text, where appropriate. Thank you, Pat, for keeping the train on the track, most of the time.

My thanks to Kit Briner, Kerry Breglia, Joanne Kant, Susan Reinhart, Bill Glass, and others, who have graciously taken the time to read some of my poems and to provide feedback and encouragement.